I0813395
cresc.

JEEYOON KIM

Beyond the Keys

MUSIC + STORIES OF INSPIRATION

GREENLEAF
BOOK GROUP PRESS

김지윤 피아니스트
pianist, Jeeyoon Kim

To.
From.

사랑하는 도훈 씨에게
이 책을 바칩니다
For Anthony

Contents

Contents

Contents

Beyond the Keys

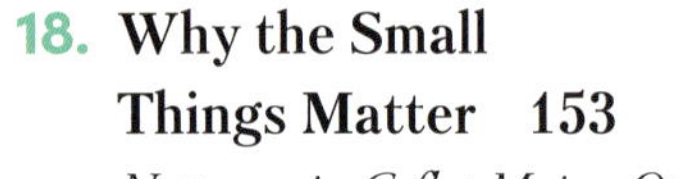

THE THIRD MOVEMENT: *LARGO APPASSIONATO*

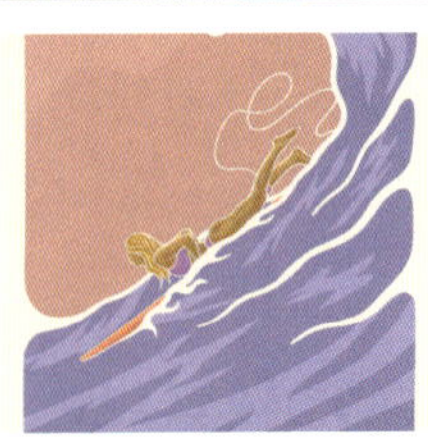

THE FOURTH MOVEMENT: *ANDANTE*

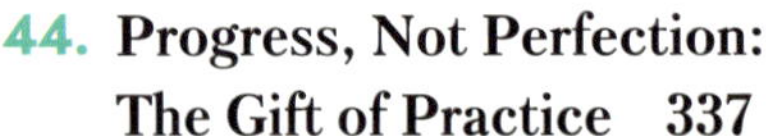

I like yellow.

Contents

Introduction

I look at myself in the mirror in the greenroom before a performance. I see someone I have known for a long time yet who remains unfamiliar. I take a deep breath from my belly.

Performance nerves play strange tricks on your mind, sometimes . . .

Ever since I started to write, something similar has been happening.

I see myself in my writing: someone whom I know intimately yet whom I have not quite figured out. Often, I see a stranger—someone it will take a long time to get to know better.

Writing started as a curiosity for me, a journey that I took to express myself. During the past four years, I have published three books: *Whenever You're Ready*, *Ever the Beginning*, and *Millions of Dreams* (백만 번의 상상, published in Korea). About five years ago, I started my biweekly newsletter, called *Behind the Keys*, for people who follow my career as a pianist, author, podcaster, teacher, and friend.

Writing has been my way of continually connecting with people and finding strength and light in my life. It has also been a tool to help me be transparent with myself in my ever-changing life.

Writing nurtures my creativity as well. Music and writing go hand in hand. Each is an intuitive and transparent activity. Just like you can't hide from your music-making, you can't hide from your writing. They both have a way of reflecting back on you, like a mirror. I've come to realize that I am a pianist who also loves to write.

I have always loved that special connection that's formed between an author and a reader—especially when an author shares their reflections on life or their authentic stories in nonfiction; I can sense things about who the author is inside, as if I know them as a close friend. Sometimes, a character in fiction makes a strong impression on me and lives in my mind for a while. It is always special for me when I experience layered emotions from a fictional character and then get to express those complex inner feelings on the piano. At times, music can fill the gap when words are no longer sufficient to express our feelings.

When I started to share my reflections on life through my newsletter, *Behind the Keys*, at first, people started to read the entries as a way to get one step closer to the pianist they decided to follow. As time went by, however, I was no longer just a pianist they followed on the internet but someone they got to know closely, someone whose life they got to experience through my diverse perspectives: the complexity of being an immigrant from South

Korea; trouble-shooting as a woman living alone in America; the variety of adventures in my travels; the struggles and joys of a concert pianist; my passion for classical music; the challenge of being an entrepreneur; ways I've overcome personal life struggles; and the everyday life of a woman in her mid-forties. Although these were my stories, they also reflected many people's life journeys.

Whenever I sent out my newsletter, people often wrote back to me saying that my writing was one of the highlights of their inbox—a dose of inspiration and positivity that they looked forward to. Sometimes, they shared their life stories with me. I could sense that this communication via words also became meaningful to them.

In the swamp of hundreds of unwanted emails we receive every week in this modern era, I felt especially grateful and humbled by people's expressions of love for my newsletter. I could tell that they genuinely meant what they said. Even though I haven't met most of my followers in person, I've become a part of their journeys through life, much like a close friend accompanies us through life.

Then, one morning, I woke up with a new idea—something I could do that would be unique.

That something was combining a book with a musical album. I would combine a musical experience of my performances through QR codes with a collection of writings from my newsletter. I would share performances from my past three albums—*10 More Minutes* (2016), *Over. Above. Beyond.* (2018), and 시음 */si-úm/* (2022)—as well as my new fourth album, *Radiance*, including *Pictures at an Exhibition* by Modest Mussorgsky.

This time, instead of releasing my new album through CD format only, I would publish this book as part of it.

I still vividly remember the morning when I had this idea for the first time. It was like getting an electric shock to my system. I couldn't wait to make this book a reality. *How long do I have to wait?* I sensed my impatience, knowing the glacial process of getting a book published. I can report that I have waited to see the completion of this project ever since that morning. Of course, time seemed to pass more slowly than usual.

But here you are, reading this, which means I did it. The project has finally become real—it's out in the world as something solid you can hold in your hand and read with your eyes *and* as sound that you can hear with your ears. Hooray! I am beyond excited to share this unique journey with you.

How This Book Works

I designed this book in such a way that each chapter will be followed by a QR code that you can use to listen to my solo piano performance. The end of each chapter concludes with a musical experience, transitioning you from the words to musical notes.

Additionally, each chapter is followed by beautiful illustrations and paintings by amazing artists from around the globe. These works of art have been created by my favorite artists. I hand selected each one to accompany my writing and music. I am honored and humbled to have collected this array of beautiful artwork for you. In these works, you will sense my love of nature, animals, and people and some of my everyday reflections.

To me, this collection is more than a book; it is a gift to you and to myself, and it's an experience we can share together. When you open this book, it can be as if you're entering a concert hall from your living room or a cute neighborhood coffee shop where we share a morning chat or an art gallery we stumble into from our walk. Wherever you are, this book can become a tool to transport you into another space. That is how the title of the book, *Beyond the Keys*, was born: To me, piano keys have been more than just musical keys; they've been a guide to a life, beyond the tool of creating music. I gaze above the current horizon, entering another spiritual realm in search of hope, with you.

This book has five movements. I followed a similar tradition of many classical composers by separating this work into different movements. Although each chapter can stand independently in this book, I had fun having a musical grouping—arranging the essays—within the book as if this were a musical composition. Many classical compositions have their Italian tempo markings next to each movement, indicating the overall mood of the musical journey. Having these essays grouped by tempo marking might help you to create a structural blueprint as you navigate the journey of this book. It is as if those tempo markings can give you the sense of a goalpost as you listen to a big-scale piece like a Mahler symphony.

The first movement of this book is in the tempo of *grave,* which is reflective, heavy, and serious, often used to convey profound emotion or gravity in a piece. Many of the essays in this movement take a close look at personal challenges, allowing me to slow down from my current pace of life and reflect.

The second movement is *allegro con brio*, which directs the performer to play at a lively tempo with energy, vigor, and a sense of brilliance or spirited enthusiasm. I shared some of my stories about overcoming daily fear and finding life's joy by doing something uncomfortable, like surfing.

The third movement is *largo appassionato*. I love music that has an *appassionato* marking attached to it. That means "passionate" in Italian. I approach each note with deep emotional intensity and passion when I play pieces in that tempo marking. It combines a sense of expansive, deliberate pacing with a heartfelt and expressive character. I hope you can find some of those emotions in the essays in this movement.

The fourth movement is *andante,* which is "at a walking pace" in music. I like this pace of music, especially because it resembles the relaxed rhythm of the heartbeat. I included some essays on my trials and errors in trying to be centered in this moment of my life rather than rushing through it.

The fifth and final movement is *presto,* commonly found in virtuosic passages or finales with excitement and energy at a quick pace. This movement has my recording of all fifteen movements of *Pictures at an Exhibition* by Modest Mussorgsky, along with the relatively shorter length of essays, so that the broader scope of the entire forty-minute performance of *Pictures at an Exhibition* can be broken into twelve different small essays and recordings. In the epilogue, you will get to hear my own composition, *10 More Minutes*, which expresses my longing for ten more minutes with you in this cherished journey of *Beyond the Keys*.

Please take your time as you move through this book. Read a chapter or two, and listen to one or two recordings. Linger over the works of art for a little while, and let them sink in, like when you stand in front of a masterpiece at a museum. Because this book is a collection of my newsletter writings over the span of the past five years, there is no hurry for you to read it all in one sitting. My wish is that the book will be an experience for you—a trail we get to walk together as a break from what you're doing.

Perhaps you will take away one or two inspirational ideas from this book.

Perhaps you will fall in love with one or two pieces from my classical music collection.

Perhaps I'll make you smile a bit from my stories.

This book is for anyone who needs a little inspiration in life. You might think of it as taking a coffee break from your busy life. First, I'll share my stories. A piano waits over there in the corner of the cafe, ready for me to play for you. This space is decorated with a beautiful collection of art on the walls, encouraging you to stop and gaze for a while.

My ultimate hope for the book is that it will shine a warm ray of sunlight on your path—just a spoonful more of strength and light to give you a pick-me-up. I am a firm believer that having any form of art, whether visual, written, or aural, enhances our life experiences. Regardless of how advanced we will become with AI technology, I doubt it will ever replace our need to create and experience art produced by other humans. For me, there will always be a longing for that human connection. Sometimes, the most healing experience we can give to ourselves is to feel, touch, read, see, and listen to a work of art.

That is what I am offering here: a connection with you through art.

I believe when we are connected through art, we develop the ability to see beyond ourselves and gain insight into a bigger perspective of the meaning of life.

It has taken me a while to become who I am now, yet I am still becoming—as are you.

It may take us an entire lifetime to transform into whatever we wish to be. We can't rush it. Life has its own timing. That is something I learned in this writing and performing process: We can't rush through life, but the wisest thing to do is to be immersed in this current moment.

Perhaps we are ultimately becoming something like a gorgeous banyan tree. Have you ever seen a picture of the mighty banyan trees in Hawaii or of someone standing in front of those giant trees? They take my breath away whenever I get near one. Each of their branches and trunks holds centuries of stories within them. I feel their sorrow, joy, pain, memories, tears, love, and strength in an all-in-one form of living. Just like that, we are continually expanding ourselves through our life experiences and transformations.

Life is an art in itself. It's the art of becoming.

I am here to share my stories and experiences of life beyond the keys. More than a pianist, I am a friend who, just as you are, is also searching for a light of life.

“Both suffering and happiness are of an organic nature, which means they are both transitory; they are always changing. The flower, when it wilts, becomes the compost. The compost can help grow a flower again. Happiness is also organic and impermanent by nature. It can become suffering and suffering can become happiness again.”

—THICH NHAT HANH

THE FIRST MOVEMENT:

Grave

1.

The Road Less Cautious

In the summer of 2000, as a sophomore undergraduate student in Korea, I decided to travel to Europe alone during my summer break. I remember the exciting moment of sharing my decision with Mom. She asked how long I would travel, and I said, "Not decided. I saved up about $1,000 and will be back when I run out of cash."

I thought this would be about a monthlong trip to Germany, Austria, or maybe Prague in the Czech Republic or other adjacent countries that I felt like visiting, depending on the whims of the moment. I purchased an open-date return airline ticket so I could fly home whenever I decided to return. I planned to visit Mozart's house and maybe where Beethoven or Schubert lived, too! I was beyond excited about this solo adventure for my first time abroad.

I carried only one backpack with minimal contents (at this point, alas, a lost skill). My first destination was Freiburg, a small city in Germany. I heard it had a great music school, and I wanted to experience a small German town. I welcomed the foreign culture: the city tram system, the smell of fresh baguettes in the morning, salami sandwiches, a street paved with small stones, and even the idea of stores that closed at 6 p.m. In Korea, everything was open till at least 2 a.m., if not twenty-four hours. The idea of closing stores this early didn't make sense to me. Where did people go after work?

Back then, there was no fancy device like a smartphone. My only navigational tool on this adventure was the travel guidebook *Lonely Planet*, which I studied every night, making notes and planning where to visit or where to stay next.

The first challenge I faced was when I visited Prague. Until then, I could easily find a room at a youth hostel without planning days in advance. Despite its beauty, this city was different from other cities in Germany. It was a bit wilder, loud, loose, and full of travelers from all over the world. On the first day, I had difficulty finding a room. The day was getting darker, and I started to become anxious. I certainly didn't want to sleep on the street. I felt tired from carrying my heavy backpack and walking all day, but I had no other choice but to knock on the doors of youth hostels one by one to see if any had a room to spare. After hours of searching late into the night, I finally found one hostel that had a single top bunk available in a dorm room of double-bunk beds.

Thank God, finally!

Walking into the dorm room, I quickly realized that I'd never experienced sleeping in a true dorm room setting in a youth hostel. About twenty double-bunk beds were lined up in a tiny room, occupied primarily by guys, most minimally clothed, resting, and chatting with each other. For a moment, I wondered if I had walked into the wrong room by mistake. I acted normal, as if this setting felt comfortable to me. In reality, I badly wanted to escape to someplace else—anywhere but here! However, considering the small budget and resources I had that night, I knew this was my best option. For the first time on this trip, I realized how brave I had been to embark on it all alone as a young girl of nineteen.

Toward the end of the two months of traveling, I counted my last few dollars. I knew the end of the trip was near. When I saw a phone booth on a sidewalk, I walked toward it and called Mom with my last international phone card, which I had saved from the beginning of the trip. With one ring, Mom picked up the phone. "Yeoboseyo?" ("hello" in Korean).

How nice to hear her voice! I felt a huge sense of relief and homesickness all at the same time. I felt tears forming, but I held them back. I didn't want Mom to worry. I realized how unconsciously I had been keeping my guard up to protect myself while I figured out everything on my own on this trip. I had been in survival mode for the last two months.

"Mom, I am ready to be back. I am tired . . ."

The truth was that I'd had an amazing experience. I had visited places that appeared to have sprung from a storybook; eaten new foods; and met adventurers, locals, and fellow travelers, who taught me how to see the world from a broader perspective. At the same time, I faced many dangerous situations from which I miraculously emerged. All my memories—good and bad—were worthwhile. I felt like I had matured at least five years during a trip of two months.

On the plane back to Korea, letting out a huge exhalation, I pondered one thing about my mom that I hadn't noticed before: She had never told me, "Be careful!" No matter how crazy something might look on the surface, such as traveling abroad alone as a young woman for two months without any solid plan, she had just let me experience it on my own. There was never a boundary that she had drawn for me beforehand. I was the one who could judge what to do in a given situation.

I realize now how unique this feature was for a parent—and as a single mom, no less. Who doesn't say "be careful" to a child?

I was thankful for who my mother was, and I was thankful that I had that freedom through which I could develop my own sense of responsibility.

The dual meaning of "be careful" is "be afraid."

How many times has each of us said this sentence, failing to realize that it could hinder our ability to explore freely?

The truth is that once one becomes a wiser individual, one

learns what healthy boundaries are for being safe or not safe. Before we say "be careful" to someone or ourselves without thinking, I would like to make some other suggestions:

> **"Let's experiment."**
> **"Let me try."**
> **"Be wise."**
> **"Be brave."**
> **"Have fun!"**

Those days of sleeping in a dorm room in a bunk bed are now a thing of the past for me. However, I am glad to have been able to experience life at that time in a style that I could have done only in my youth. I am thankful I bravely opened that door without the phrase "be careful" holding me back.

Concert Corner

Concert Étude No. 6, "Pastoral," Op. 40 by Nikolai Kapustin

2.

What Was It Like Performing at Carnegie Hall?

I write this in my hotel room on Jeju Island, South Korea, listening to a wild ocean. The rainy season is about to start here in Korea. The humid air with a warm summer breeze feels strangely familiar, a sensation from my youth. However, this stormy weather won't affect my tour in Korea, which starts today. It's hard to believe that I am on the other side of the world after having had such an intense week in New York City performing just days ago at the iconic Carnegie Hall.

"What was it like performing at Carnegie Hall?"

First, let me rewind to the times before playing at the Carnegie, as performers call it. As fancy and exciting as it may sound, preparing for this concert wasn't an easy task—physically, mentally, or emotionally. Aside from strategically practicing each piece for hours every day, I had to work through my chatty mind that distracted my focus. The name *Carnegie* would make any musician nervous about standing on such a historical stage. I worked hard for my mind to be in a space where I would be grounded and ready to accept whatever would be.

I perform all the time, but it always amazes me that performing never gets easier over time. Just like life, each new day challenges me to renew my approach to what is important to me as a pianist and as a person.

Focus. Gratitude. Letting go. Flow. Accepting. Joy. Love. Gift. Celebration. Grounding. Openness. Now.

These are the words I collected to remind me to recenter myself over the months of preparation for the concert. Each word came to me at a random insightful moment, and then I practiced holding the word in the palm of my hand to keep it alive within me.

The day of the performance had the worst air quality on record in New York because of a wildfire in Canada. The city was full of smoke at two o'clock in the afternoon, making everything look yellow and fuzzy. Walking through the crowds to my rehearsal in an unusually dark light at that hour, I felt like I was watching a documentary about a natural disaster in slow motion. Noticing my unease, I said to myself, *I am going to play at the Carnegie tonight. I am sure there will be some people who will make it. Nothing can stop me now. Stay calm and focused.*

Stepping into the hall after going through many layers of

security, I was surprised to see the hall again. It was gorgeous and elegant, even more magnificent than I remembered. Then, with a hint of nervousness and excitement, I sat down and played several pieces on the shiny Steinway on the stage.

I instantly felt goosebumps on my arms and said to myself, *Ah, this piano is amazing. It allows me to do anything I could ask for, from a delicate, velvety tone of various colors to thunderous sound. The hall is just big enough to hug the sound, giving back the warmth of the space. This could well be the best piano I've ever played.*

I've experienced many wonderful pianos, but I've often found that they fall short in one way or another. What seems to be a beautiful-looking nine-foot Steinway onstage frequently has underlying health conditions that pianists must work extra hard to cover up. I have accepted that this is a part of the work that we have to deal with as pianists. After all, we don't carry our own instruments (unless you are extremely lucky, like Vladimir Horowitz, who got to travel with his piano).

Some pianos have great bass tones and big power overall, yet they lack the shiny melodic tone of the upper register and the sensitivity of touch. Or they might have a great clarity of sound, but the action is too heavy to play a light, fast, glossy passage. Or a piano has one too many tones that stick out from the rest of the notes. When that is the case, I make a mental note of which ones are louder than the others and make sure I play more softly whenever my fingers go to those notes. (This particular condition is a lot of extra work, which pianists hate to deal with.) As a result, onstage, pianists not only have to concentrate on the music, techniques, and expression but also cover the weaknesses of the piano and make the most out of its strengths.

What is interesting to me is that after years of experience playing hundreds of different pianos, I now expect a certain unique weakness in any given instrument. However, what I also learned is that if I give all my energy to create the best out of whatever-condition piano I encounter, most of the time, they do produce a sound far beyond their initially evaluated capacity. Just like people, pianos need pianists who trust them to do the best they can; then, they stretch themselves magically when the spotlight is on them with that encouragement.

Does a piano never limit me in any way? That is certainly rare. Yet the piano at Carnegie Hall was possibly the only time that one gave me so much freedom to simply fly with my music. On top of that, when paired with a good acoustic hall and the significance of sharing the moment with an appreciative audience in a space like the Carnegie, it was a nearly impossible combination to duplicate.

(As a side note, the piano on which I performed at my Carnegie debut in 2017 wasn't at this level. Yes, it was an amazing instrument. But compared to this particular instrument—the piano I encountered in 2017—it didn't come close to the range of colors, evenness of action, and adaptivity of different styles of the repertoire. This piano was just two years young and in its best shape. If I return to the Carnegie, the piano could be different again. But that night in Carnegie Hall, the instrument was the best I could ever hope for as a pianist.)

When I finally walked onstage towards an enthusiastic crowd that night, I spotted familiar faces who had traveled from San Diego and, of course, my mom from Korea. But the majority of the audience members were New Yorkers whom I didn't know. An hour-and-a-half-long concert felt like five minutes to me—a total focus on existence. During the performance, I kept reminding myself to stay in the moment, let go of even my wish to do my best, and be open and curious. As the night went on, I felt I could lean on the present moment more and more firmly. I knew that the pressure of the weight of the space, the Carnegie, would not go away, no matter when I played there. But I am most proud that in the end, I could soar above the weight of its significance.

The next morning, an official review in the *New York Classical Review* came out. Rick Perdian titled it "The Musical and Personal Are Closely Twined with Pianist Jeeyoon Kim," mentioning "impeccable technique, consummate musicianship, and communicative skills as a pianist." Another reviewer, Leonid Goldin, wrote in Russian, "The pianist's performing skills produced a very strong impression . . . The audience in Carnegie Hall does not always give a standing ovation even at the end of the concert; this time, they got up after almost every piece—in my opinion, a well-deserved assessment."

So to give a long answer (to the question "what's it like to play in Carnegie Hall?"), in short, I say this: As I looked at the crowd from the stage after the second encore while I walked off and went backstage, the one word that rang out to me was *thankful*. I was thankful for this night, thankful for friends who were there for me, thankful for enthusiastic crowds, thankful for the opportunity, thankful for the piano, thankful for music, thankful for my drive to keep pushing, thankful for my health, and thankful to be alive at that moment. It was certainly a high point in my life, and I was filled with gratitude.

After a concert, I always feel I have become someone different. The rich experience allows me to dig deeper into myself and my life, and I always come out feeling a bit more grounded. As rigorous as the preparation for each concert, whenever I return to my piano bench to start my daily practice, I find myself looking forward to sharing another musical journey with you.

Piano Sonata in Op. 27, No. 2, "Moonlight," by Ludwig van Beethoven

Silent Luminosity by Kaoru Yamada

The Untold Story

Growing up, I was Daddy's girl. I remember running toward the entrance to our house at full speed, with a big smile, at the slightest sound of the door. I showered him with bear hugs and kisses whenever he returned home or left for work. I always giggled at his silly jokes, as if nothing else mattered in this world. As he always told me, I was the sunshine of his life.

He was a soft-spoken and artistic person. In spring, he would take me to the riverside to pick wildflowers by the handfuls. He always asked me to accompany him on his errands, telling me that everything was more fun when I was with him. He was strict about certain things, though, such as that I could never have a sleepover at my friend's house or that I needed to learn to eat a piece of kimchi—spicy pickled cabbage—at every meal. I remember gulping one tiny piece of kimchi with a big spoonful of white rice without chewing. That was my clever tactic not to taste kimchi. (Luckily, I finally learned to love kimchi.) In my eyes, he was like a superhero. I felt special, cared for, and loved by him.

One day in my first year of high school, Mom told me, out of nowhere, that she would have to divorce Dad. She had been waiting for me to grow up enough to understand the situation and had already packed her belongings. Mom told me Dad had had an affair with his secretary, which had gone on for decades. That day, my picture-perfect world turned upside down.

"There must have been some misunderstanding here"—that is what Dad said to me. Perhaps Mom has been overreacting to some things, and there was a major miscommunication. Dad confirmed that whatever I had heard was not accurate.

I believed him one hundred percent. I was sure he would tell me the truth. *Of course he would.*

However, without Mom, the house was never the same. Everything felt too quiet and unusual in the comfort of my home, as if I were in the opening scene of a film in which a disaster was about to strike.

Mom stayed temporarily at Grandma's house while my parents settled the divorce. It was not as simple as I had thought. This divorce process included both parties hiring private investigators, freezing their assets so neither could move, and proving each other wrong in court battles, one after the other. This was not a peaceful sign-off. They intended to follow the script: "Let's fight to find out who will be the last one standing." Indeed, this battle lasted for four years without any clear winners.

As a freshman in my art high school, it was difficult to cope with this change in my personal life while juggling the competitive nature of being a piano major and studying hard for other academic courses. Taking private piano lessons was very expensive at that time in Korea, but I needed to improve to get into a good university.

One day, about six months after Mom left home, Dad asked me if I would consider changing my path, to major in either pharmacy or medicine at university, perhaps changing my high school, too. "You are such a great student," he said. "Why not work toward something where you could earn more money than playing the piano?"

The actual message I heard underneath was, *It is costly for me to support your music. Why don't you change to something cheaper?*

That was difficult for me because I could not think of anything besides music. That passion has been loud and clear to me all my life (thank God . . .).

That was when I had to make a dramatic decision: to leave my dad to be with Mom for now. Just for now. Plus, he would be on just the other side of the city, only thirty minutes away.

This wasn't about taking sides, but I chose the piano. I thought it was just a temporary condition to leave Dad until everything became more transparent for everyone.

I couldn't bring myself to tell my father in person, so I wrote him a letter. On my last night with him, knowing I'd be leaving him in the morning, I cried hard in bed, quietly under the blanket. I felt heartbroken to leave him just like that. I felt the pain in my chest for him and myself. By the time he read that letter, I had already left him.

Surely, this is not the end. I will see him soon enough.

I don't know what I thought, but I just assumed I would see him soon enough after that night—maybe a week? Maybe a month? Surely not four years of my entire high school or another four years of my undergraduate years in Korea.

I waited for him to visit me at my high school. *Maybe he will come and tell me everything is okay and he still loves me.*

Eventually, after eight years, both in high school and as an undergraduate, waiting turned into deep sadness. That sadness turned into confusion. That confusion turned into anger. That anger turned into indifference. Each course of my emotional roller coaster, I wondered if I were to bump into him on a street, what I would say and how I would greet him. *Do I say hello? Do I ignore him? Would he even be able to recognize me?*

I actually had one phone conversation with him—only one. I was a senior in high school. He had called to ask me to play the piano at his wedding. He was getting married to the secretary that Mom accused him of being with. He said to me, "My daughter is a pianist. Why would I go elsewhere?" At first, I said I would. (I don't know what I was thinking.) Several days later, I called and said I couldn't do it. (To this day, Mom is still angry about this request.) The wedding would take place several weeks before a big university entrance exam. I couldn't imagine going through such an emotional event before that exam.

Fast-forward to several weeks before I left for America to earn my master's degree in piano performance at Indiana University. I was no longer a little girl but had become a young woman—without seeing Dad once during those eight years of my life. I packed everything for the big move abroad and was all ready to go, except for one task, a task that I could finally see myself performing: meeting Dad face to face. I would tell him how disappointed I was. I would tell him, "In fact, I didn't need you in my life, and I grew up fine without you. You are a liar."

After a simple, dry conversation about scheduling a meeting, we agreed to meet at a cafe. In the meantime, for days, I rehearsed my lines about what I would say to him. I was ready to tell him everything: my pain, sadness, anger, and disappointment.

My nerves grew jittery as I waited for him to arrive at the cafe. Then came the sound of the door opening—*ding ding*—and there he was. He walked toward me with a big warm smile, as he used to give me when I was little, running toward him.

That was when I broke down. An unexpected burst of tears poured down my face. All of the memorized lines and all of the sentences that I might have uttered, intending to hurt him, were gone. The only thing I felt was how much I'd missed him.

Much more than I had thought.

Maybe he was older. I noticed different lines on his face. Perhaps

I had become taller, or he became shorter . . . One way or another, it was simply lovely for me to see him. That was all. Nothing else mattered at that moment.

We hugged and cried together for a while.

Then, after a bit, he finally calmed himself and said, "How could you leave me like that? You were everything for me. I can't believe you left me behind like that. You hurt me deeply, and I am still wounded by it."

That was the first thing he said.

It was not how much he missed me, was sorry, or loved me or how good it was to see me. It was about his wound, and he was accusing me of causing it.

For the first time in my life, I was able to see who he really was. He wasn't my superhero anymore but someone who couldn't see others' pain, someone who wrapped his mind only around himself.

I learned from this process that everyone's story is unique to their mind. I no longer assume my story would be perceived by someone else in the same way.

That means I could not honestly know and understand others' views either. If I could try to live someone else's life for a moment, however, as stories allow us to, I could do a somewhat better job of empathizing with others in that fleeting moment.

If I try to put myself in my dad's mind, I can relate to him and understand myself. Both of us were searching for a deep sense of belonging and love, making mistakes, getting lost in life somewhere, and finding meaning again. We were just being human.

I don't keep in contact with Dad now. However, I am forever indebted to him for allowing me to have a real Superman in my life and for the beautiful memories from my childhood that shaped who I am now in a positive light.

Concert Corner

Waltz in C-sharp Minor, Op. 64, No. 2 by Frédéric Chopin

The Cat Who Taught Me to Love and Let Go

I recently stumbled on a world of storytelling and read the amazing book *Storyworthy* by Matthew Dicks. (I *highly* recommend it!) This book is full of wisdom and the value of telling stories. I find that storytelling is one of the strongest forms of connection with others and, most importantly, with ourselves. Yesterday was National Cat Day, and I thought I would tell you a story about Pong Pong—a cat I met in 2007.

I was practicing the piano in my apartment on a nice spring morning in Bloomington, Indiana. I was in my doctorate program at the University of Indiana, and practicing for long hours in my apartment was part of my daily routine. My apartment was in a one-story building, and I could see out of the window from the piano bench, which I always loved. That day, I noticed a ginger cat walking on the grass in the corner of the building. I didn't pay much attention at first; then, I noticed that he always visited at a certain time, mostly while I was playing the piano. He was regular enough to make me feel like I was actually giving him a concert. He sat under the sun in the distance for a while as if he had come to listen to the music.

When I grew up in Korea, cats were always culturally seen as wild, often dangerous, and never as pets. Because of this upbringing, I felt a distance from cats without much general knowledge of their characteristics. Yet, at the same time, I found myself intrigued by this orange creature that came into my world in Indiana. I started to look forward to the moment when he would show up. Sometimes, I sat outside looking for him for hours. I always smiled the moment the orange coat appeared from the bushes. *There he is!* Although I could tell he was also intrigued by my existence, he would always sit far from me. We often looked at each other for a while without taking any action.

One day, he decided to come a little closer, still keeping his suspicious look. I thought about various ways to earn his trust: I threw a treat I had bought for him into the distance. He seemed to like it by eating everything, even after careful observation. I sat still without much movement. Throwing treats at a distance was my way of letting him know I was not a threat to him but a friend who wanted to get to know him better. Little by little, the distance between us got closer and closer.

It still took three solid months for him to come within a foot from me and finally eat some wet canned food I'd prepared. The first time I could actually pet him was a moment of breakthrough. He welcomed my gentle touch and leaned his body against my legs. He had beautiful green eyes. I named him Pong Pong, which means "trampoline" in Korean. He reminded me of the pure joy I had with a trampoline growing up. I felt our friendship became official when I gave him a name.

He showed up almost every day except some rainy days. Once he accepted me as his friend, he also decided to extend himself as my roommate. He proudly came inside my apartment and kept me company on the chair next to the piano while I was practicing. On a rare occasion, he even sat on my lap. However, this didn't mean he would live with me. He always kept his street life. At a certain time, he always asked me to open the front door so he could leave. As much as I wanted to ask him to stay, I didn't feel I had the right to hold him back. He was a free spirit, and I didn't have any intention of changing that. I had to learn to let him go even though I was always happy to see him whenever he came to visit.

That relationship lasted almost a year. Then, one day, he didn't show up. Then, he didn't show up the next day or the day after that. These were beautiful autumn days with gentle sunlight, which was his favorite kind of weather, but Pong Pong was not to be seen. He stopped showing up, just like that. I started to have an uneasy feeling about it. Maybe he had an accident; maybe he fell sick. A million thoughts came through my head, causing me to worry about him all day. I had nightmares about him getting hit by a car. *Please be well, Pong Pong . . .*

After about two weeks, I decided to put posters around the neighborhood to see whether anyone had found him. I didn't have much faith in the posters, but I had no other way to find him otherwise. Maybe some neighbors had seen him around and knew him, too.

Miraculously, the next day, I got a call from a guy telling me that he seemed to know the cat. I was ecstatic to hear the news and felt relief in my chest. He said he knew where this cat was, adding, "The picture looks awfully like my cat." I didn't register what he meant at first; then, I realized that I actually didn't know anything about Pong Pong. He could have an owner! That thought just never crossed my mind.

I asked the guy whether I could visit his house to see "his" cat. He said it would be no problem. His house was just two blocks from mine in the same apartment complex. As I walked toward his unit, I noticed my heart was pounding fast. I couldn't tell whether I was nervous or excited. I timidly knocked on his door twice. When the front door opened, there he was: The beautiful ginger cat, my Pong Pong, was peacefully sleeping on someone else's couch.

I don't know what I was feeling, but initially, I was mostly relieved that he was safe. *Thank God!* I thought. I didn't share details about my relationship with Pong Pong with the owner. I briefly said I had noticed the orange cat around the complex, but I hadn't seen him for a while and worried that something happened to the cat. I honestly don't remember what I exactly said to the guy. Words didn't make any sense in my head because I was in shock. I quickly wrapped up our short conversation, thanked him for showing me his cat, and headed out in a hurry.

Pong Pong looked different in that space. He went by a totally different name. The most confusing part was that he acted indifferent to my appearance. I think I felt every emotion in the world at that moment, maybe anger, maybe sadness, disappointment—yet also relief, peace, and happiness. As I walked home, I wiped the tears coming down my face. *It is okay. He is safe. That is what matters the most.*

I learned a great lesson from this unique experience: to love something unconditionally, then, at the same time, is to let go of that attachment and be able to laugh. Mr. Double-Life Pong Pong! He never came back to my apartment. Underneath my apparent emotion of missing having him around (especially when I was practicing piano), I was happy to know that he was safe, and I knew we could always cherish our beautiful memories together.

One thing is for sure: I became a cat person.

Concert Corner

"Je te veux" by Erik Satie

The Potted Guardian by Kaoru Yamada

Choose the Light

It was an intuitive decision when I decided to get married at age twenty-nine. Everyone around me, including Mom, was surprised to hear that I was engaged at that relatively young age compared with other friends in my circle. Many assumed that I would marry late or never because of my passion for music. When I met Max (alias) in my mid-twenties at the music school, we were instantly attracted to each other, sharing a passion for piano and our lives as music students. I loved his warm, loving personality and intelligence. Not to mention he was the first person to help me get over my wounds from the difficult relationship with my dad.

After dating for two years, we got married and settled in Indianapolis—in a new two-story house in a cute neighborhood where we could walk to restaurants and shops. Everything felt like it was meant to be, and we sensed a happy future ahead of us.

Until that day when everything turned the other way around.

Earlier that week, Max seemed a bit more agitated than usual. He stayed up all night working on the computer. He had become a skilled computer programmer and was working for a big company. He said some unusual activity was occurring on his computer, as though a hacker from a foreign country had tried to get inside his desktop. He seemed amused yet disturbed, at the same time, about having to monitor this illegal action. I gave him more space than usual that week as he sorted out the situation. I remember he stayed up almost five days straight without much sleep.

On Saturday evening that week, around 10 p.m., Max breathlessly asked me to come downstairs to where he stood by the window. As I walked toward him, I noticed that he looked alarmed. He whispered into my ear, "Someone is out there by that blue car. He is watching us right now. He might try to break into the house."

I looked outside. Without a streetlight, it was hard to see anything clearly. "Really?" I asked. "Should I call the police?"

"No. I will monitor the situation here by the window," he replied. "Turn off all the lights inside the house."

My heart raced. By his demeanor, it was clear that Max was certain that something terrible was lurking outside. I sat down quietly in the corner of the living room. Then, I noticed the big knife that Max clutched in his hand as he stared agitatedly out the window. "Don't worry," he whispered. "I will protect you from that guy."

That was the moment when a different thought came into my mind.

Is it possible that he is seeing things that I don't see? Could this be a psychotic episode? Is he losing his mind?

Suddenly, I felt unsafe being in the house alone with my husband. My hands shook with fear. I knew he would never harm me, but if something terrible were to happen, I wouldn't know what to do. I decided to call my parents-in-law to come over as soon as they could. They said it would take about three hours to drive, but they would come immediately.

By the time my in-laws arrived at 2 a.m., Max was pacing around the house, fully exhausted from the anxiety. I had told him that his parents were coming to protect us and—from a distance—calmed him down as much as I could.

As soon as they walked into the house, my father-in-law said to Max, "Give me everything you have taken. You went too far. No more. This needs to stop."

Wait. What is he talking about?

The next thing I learned was a hard truth, one that I had been blind to and wouldn't have seen in a million years: Max was a drug addict who had been trapped in hard drugs—from narcotics, cocaine, and meth to everything else imaginable in that world—for years. Apparently, for a while, he could be a "functional" addict—until he couldn't function anymore.

The next few weeks or months remain a blur. I felt like I had been hit by a truck and then found myself at the bottom of the ocean, drowning, unable to see any light. Max's parents and I were deeply connected, like fellow soldiers in a brutal battle scene. We cried together and checked in with each other. We would do everything we could to turn this around. He would go to rehab. He would have to go through a difficult stage of his life to get clean. We would be there for him. I would help him get through it.

The problem was that Max didn't want any of this. He insisted he was okay. He said he had everything under control. He refused to go to rehab. He said he could handle it on his own.

Once I found myself dropped into this world of drugs, everything made sense, and I understood why I hadn't noticed the many red flags that Max had been flying all along. Having grown up in Korea, which used to be a drug-free country, this was simply my blind spot.

After a while, I gave him an ultimatum: "Max, choose me or the drugs. One or the other. They can't coexist. Just choose one."

Honestly, I thought he would be on his knees to beg me to stay. Honestly, I thought he would say he'd messed up but he would do anything to change—for him and, just as importantly, for us.

Instead, he said, "I am so sorry. I can't."

He couldn't choose me over the drugs. At the end of the day, I was not important enough for him to fight for. I was in shock. *Is this a real life?* I felt like I had been stabbed in my heart all over again. That meant the end of us, the end of this marriage, which meant I would have to leave him or he would leave me.

At the same time, I knew, for once, that Max was being truly honest with himself—for the moment. It would have been a lie for him to choose me over the drugs. At that moment, he told me his truthful choice.

The next day, I left the house with a few belongings and temporarily got a room at the home of a couple I found from a quick Craigslist search.

I cried every day for months. Some days, I was surprised at how much liquid I could retain in my body. It felt like I had an unstoppable fountain that could continually generate tears.

The bottom that I thought Max had hit months before was never the bottom for him. He lost his wife, his house, his car, his credit rating, his health, his integrity, his love of music, and everything about him. He dug the hole he lived in ever deeper as the days and months passed.

One day, I got a phone call from Max, who asked if he could borrow $30 for gas. He sounded drugged. He sounded like someone I didn't know. I would have given him $3,000—no, $30,000—if he needed something important, but I couldn't give him that $30. That was something I couldn't give. That was just another trap for me to enable him to do something worse. I bit my tongue, said I couldn't give him the money, and hung up.

I cried out loud all night after that phone call, as if my heart were bursting out of my body. The sound of my crying was raw, like that of an animal. In the midst of that pain, only one thought occupied my mind: *Don't die, Max. Don't kill yourself. Live. Please live. Choose light.*

The divorce process was unbearably simple: Sign the paper, and mail the document to the court. I lost someone I loved just like that. I lost someone I dreamed of growing old with. Yet that person didn't even exist in this world anymore and was unable to feel our loss. I wished I could fight against someone. I wished I could scream at the other opponent in this battle, but no one was in the fighting ring. All the loss and heartache were mine to take alone—a solo journey.

I honestly didn't feel betrayed by Max. Although he had hidden his addiction from me for a long time, I didn't feel angry. All I felt was a sincere wish for him not to die and not to ruin his life more than he had done. I wanted to slap him or shake him hard until he woke up from the fantasy that he was caught in. *Why would you throw your good life away like that? Wake up, wake up, wake up! Please . . .*

He had been in the darkness for years. As many people expected, he was eventually imprisoned for several years for one reason or another. To be honest, to me, being in prison sounded much better than being ensnared by drugs. *Time away from the real world could be his saving grace to turn things around.*

More than a decade has passed since then. A few months ago, I heard great news: He has remained clean after being released from prison and is now back in the world with a decent job. He also found someone he loves and will soon marry. When I heard this, I let out a big sigh of relief that I had been holding for years.

I don't keep in contact with him, and I don't plan to do so, because my memories of our time together are too tender, no matter how much time has passed. However, my thoughts about him have always been the same: I wish him well. I wish him to be happy and healthy. *Please choose light. Fight for your life.*

From this experience, my eyes were opened to the extreme difficulties faced by the families and friends of addicts. No matter what I have been through, I still don't know what I could have done differently in those impossible circumstances.

However, one truth remains that has saved me in the dark tunnel.

"This, too, shall pass."

Time heals. I sit here enjoying the warm sun rays by the ocean. The sound of waves is soothing. I smile gently.

Life has offered me many lemons, but I've managed to make many flavors of lemonade from them. If anything at all, this has taught me to become much more empathetic than I otherwise might be.

I am sure you have bitten into your fair share of lemons, too.

Still, life is worth fighting for.

Concert Corner

Chaconne in G Major, HWV 435
by George Frideric Handel

The Leafy Embrace by Shin Jinho

6.

It Doesn't Have to Be Good or Bad

I was driving along a country road surrounded by big trees. The various shades of vibrantly colored leaves gave me the feeling of being inside a beautiful autumn painting. For long stretches, I saw neither people nor cars. Mesmerized by the beauty of the scenic ride, I noticed a huge black object in the middle of the dusty road. From a distance, it looked like a big black bear lying on the ground. As I stopped my car in the middle of the road near the animal, I realized that it was a large fluffy black dog; it was sleeping. There was no way I could drive around it on the narrow country road, so I rolled my window down and poked my head out. "Hello, there!" I called out. "How are you?"

He shook his body sideways several times and slowly got up, glancing at me from the sides of his eyes. His demeanor made me chuckle. Then, he walked slowly toward the driver's side to my window, wagging his tail. He didn't look at all dangerous—more like a teddy bear that could use a good bath. He voluntarily put his head on my hand, asking me to pet him.

"Hi, baby," I said. "You are a good boy. Thank you for saying hello."

After a good minute of us exchanging greetings, he moved his body away from the window to allow me to pass . . . finally. I slowly started the car. In the rearview mirror, I could see him ambling back to the position in the middle of the road and flopping his body to the ground.

When I arrived at Knob Creek, the nickname of this farmhouse in Indiana, about twenty chickens were busy running around, finding bugs in the weeds. Linda opened the front door excitedly and came outside onto the patio. She shouted, "Welcome, Fruit Monkey! Did you see the 'speed bump' on your way? The big black fluffy dog that wouldn't let you pass unless he gets a pet?"

"Hello, Mutti!" I laughed. "Ha ha, yes! I sure did!"

I could smell some yummy food in the oven with crackling sounds from the fire in the fireplace. *This feels like home . . .* We decided to walk to the end of the country road and back before dinner. The walk would take about thirty minutes, she said. Her two Border collie dogs, Toss and Penny, and a black cat named Oscar and a gray one named Felix joined our walk with Father Fish

(Linda's husband; we call him FF). These country cats behaved like dogs. "Cats always join our evening walk," Linda said as Oscar ran in front of us, meowing playfully.

As a side note, we have nicknames for each other at Knob Creek. I am not sure how it all started, but mine came from how much I loved eating fruit and how much volume I could consume in one sitting. The way I picked blackberries from the bush and ate in their backyard reminded my friends of a monkey who loves fruit, so I became Fruit Monkey for them.

After walking for five minutes, we approached the entrance to another residence. As we got closer, three dogs jumped up happily and ran toward us—a big brown one, a medium-sized short-haired one, and a small fluffy white one. The way they wagged their tails wildly made me think they knew our pack of animals, including us. As we continued our walk, I noticed all three dogs joined our walk, as if this had been agreed on in advance.

Then, at another house entrance five minutes later, another dog ran toward us, also wagging his tail. So far, we had seen no signs of a human on this walk. However, each time we walked past the entrance to a group of four houses, more dogs joined us. At one point, looking behind us, I felt like we were in some Disney movie, having an adventure with ten animals of all sizes. Interestingly, some seemed to be best friends, playing with each other and zooming through the crowd we had made; others seemed annoyed that they had to walk, but still they followed. No one had asked them to join us, but they all did voluntarily.

When we arrived at the end of the road, where thicker woods started, we decided to turn around. Even more amusingly, as soon as we arrived at each dog's entrance to their house, they all returned to their homes without saying goodbye. I shouted to their backs, "Bye! Have a good night!" By the time we returned to the farmhouse, we were back to our original count of two dogs, two cats, and three humans.

In the morning, I was awakened by a rooster's loud crowing and a particular sound of birds: "Whip-poor-will, whip-poor-will!" *This is way better than modern alarm clock technology. There is no way one could sleep through these sounds.* I wasn't sure what time it was, but I was fully awake thanks to the liveliness of creatures preparing for the new day. (Afterward, I found out it was 5:30 a.m.) Linda and I went to the chicken coop for fresh eggs and to pick greens from the garden. She baked sourdough bread from scratch, which filled the house with the warm aroma of fresh bread. In a warm sweater and with a fresh cup of coffee, I cozied up on a couch by the fire.

More than fifteen years have passed since I first experienced Knob Creek.

When I drove back to Knob Creek several weeks ago, I slowed my car way down at the spot where "the speed bump" used to lie, waiting to be petted. He had passed away years ago, but I could see him vividly in my mind's eye. I realized that I was pausing in the middle of the road for no reason, and I returned to driving. *Ah, I miss him . . .*

This is Knob Creek—the home of my former in-laws.

The last time I had a concert in Indiana, I told my close friend that I would visit my ex-in-laws and stay overnight at their house. She asked me, "Is it good for you that you keep in close contact with them? Doesn't it make it difficult for you to go back there after that emotionally difficult divorce?"

I pondered that question for a while. Maintaining this close relationship with my ex-in-laws might look a bit out of the norm from the outside, indeed.

Then, I realized something else: Not everything that happens to us has to be defined as good or bad. Sometimes, in life, it just is.

I feel a deep sense of connection to my former in-laws. I feel like we are fellow soldiers who have survived a brutal battle. We share a sense of having lost someone whom we loved deeply and a loss of unity as a family. Whenever I go back, I must admit that there is always a puddle of emotion from which ripples try to arise from below. Sometimes, it is not easy. Yet, at the same time, we exist once again in this special place, Knob Creek, sharing our love without any labels of who we are.

Whenever I am at Knob Creek, I am reminded that I can be here and now, surrounded by love and nature. I am thankful to have had a beautiful experience and fond memories that deepen my existence in this life.

Concert Corner

Intermezzo in A Major, Op. 118, No. 2 by Johannes Brahms

Puppy Train Play by Gobom

7.

Rise Above the Distractions

A casual conversation I had with a friend last week brought up the interesting topic of distraction. We talked about how much we are bombarded with noise, information, and, most notoriously, our attachment to our phones as we keep checking text messages, emails, YouTube, and other social media.

My friend said he is conflicted as he enjoys using his phone but doesn't like spending much time on it. He said, "It *is* fun. It is like how a hungry kid feels at a buffet. What do you do with all of these yummy foods in front of you? Just ignore them and eat moderately? Given the limitations of normal human willpower, a phone is designed to make us lose the balance of life."

This conversation made me think of my trials and errors in

easing my attachment to my phone. I feel I am losing my sense of direction because I depend heavily on the phone for driving directions. I check my emails when I take breaks during piano practice and enjoy watching my favorite YouTube channels when I want some quick entertainment.

As much as I like the convenience of a smartphone, I am also mindful that this little thing can be a source of distraction and a Zen breaker.

When I practice piano, I often record myself so I can listen and offer myself constructive feedback. It is never easy, especially at an early stage of performance practice. After a while, though, by setting my feelings aside, I can eventually see myself in the video as another person. I can observe from the video which part I should work on and how to plan for my next practice session.

I tried a similar process with my phone. I used the *Offscreen* app, which monitors how long you use your phone, the duration of each app usage, and how many times you pick up your phone each day. I was especially surprised and embarrassed at the same time when I saw the number for the frequency of my phone pickups in a day go as high as forty or fifty times. *Do I really pick it up that often?*

That is when I decided to try something new to change my habit.

They say the only way to combat distraction is to have a solid plan in advance. Even if you don't follow the plan exactly, you can at least define the task you want to focus on and pinpoint what distracts you at any given time.

I think the biggest problem with excessive phone usage is that you're letting your phone control your time. Even though you might start with the intention of using your phone only during a short break, the phone is a genius at keeping your attention on the things you like. One minute of cute cat or dog videos can easily turn into thirty to forty-five minutes away from what you intended to do in the first place.

Here are some of my ongoing trials and errors in this battle that have worked fairly well for me thus far.

1. Know *why* you don't want to use your phone as much as you currently do. My first reason is to avoid tiring my eyes, which I experience from using a computer screen or phone; I need a greener landscape for my overworked eyes. Second, I want to train my brain to focus more deeply, because the ability to have a deep and immersive experience at any moment is important for me, and I know excessive phone usage can diminish that deep-focus ability.

2. Monitor your usage objectively. How long do you use your phone? How often do you use it? Which app is the most time-consuming?

3. Set limits to your phone usage that you can stick to. In my case, I try not to use my phone until an hour after I wake up and an hour before going to bed as a bare minimum boundary. Since this was initially difficult for me to do, I used the help of the *Opal* app. I set a lock for my phone so that I'm unable to use certain apps at specific times. For

example, I locked my email app from 9:30 p.m. to 8 a.m. the next day. During that time, app icons appear gray, with a lock sign. You can unlock your phone anytime through the app, but that extra step discourages me from doing so. I have also heard positive reviews of the *Freedom, Offscreen,* and *Jomo* apps, which have similar functions. I plan to experiment with these apps in the future.

4. Check your email at a set time, or at least less often than you do now. I don't know when we started treating emails as instant text messages. You don't have to read each email as soon as it appears in your inbox; people can most likely wait a day or two for your reply.

5. Charge your phone farther away from your bed or, better yet, in another room, if possible.

6. Try a phone-free dinner outing, concert, or walk. Leave your phone in another room while practicing playing the piano or when you need to focus deeply on your task. (Thankfully, this is the easiest step for me. I can always leave a phone in the car before going to the restaurant or concert.)

7. Play with a color. For example, when I want less stimulation, I make the entire screen on my iPhone appear in grayscale mode by clicking the "Menu" button three times consecutively. In addition, I set my phone mostly to the less bright "Night Shift" color mode even in the daytime to reduce the strain on my eyes.

8. Use the "Do Not Disturb" function to your advantage. I use this most of the day. I never hear nor see a notification from any app, including for spam calls. I set it in such a way that I can still receive emergency calls or other important calls from people I've added to my "Favorites" list.

For a while, I have wanted to go to some kind of silent retreat, somewhere peaceful in nature. I thought it would be wonderful to disconnect and experience tranquility in that special environment. I might feel rejuvenated or enlightened. Then again, perhaps all I wanted was to disconnect myself from Wi-Fi more often to be able to focus more deeply.

Maybe the real silent retreat can happen right here in my living room whenever I wish.

I just have to turn off my phone.

Concert Corner

Coda alla Reminiscenza, Op. 38, No. 8 from
Forgotten Melodies by Nikolai Medtner

Verdant Tranquility by Kaoru Yamada

Crying Over a Student

I vividly remember my first piano teacher when I was four years old. Every afternoon at about two o'clock, I grabbed my piano bag and went out the door alone. As my parents were busy with their work, going to a piano institute as a four-year-old was my only responsibility, which I took seriously.

On the exterior, the piano institute looked like a residential home, but inside, there were many small rooms, and in each room was a piano. The floors were wooden, and we took our shoes off as we entered. Each day when I arrived at the institute, my piano instructor greeted me with a warm smile. Even though she might have been in the middle of another lesson, she made sure to talk to me and check that I knew which piano room I should go into. Once I sat down at a piano, I started with a finger exercise called "Hanon."

I honestly don't remember much of what I did other than sporadic memories of scenes in the piano institute and the music I played. However, I remember how she made me feel during those lessons; she always supported me and made me feel loved.

When I first started my undergraduate studies in Korea, teaching piano on the side was a luxurious resource that not all university students had. At the first opportunity to teach five-year-olds in my freshman year, I happily took the job. I thought to myself, *I have been playing piano for fifteen years, already with an advanced repertoire. How difficult could it be to teach a five-year-old beginner?*

In our first lesson, I went to the student's house with the excitement of starting something new. However, unlike my perfect plan for the first lesson of teaching a prodigy who could do everything I asked, the reality was that I was teaching a kid who was not interested in piano, accompanied by a dog and a cat whose main motives seemed to be disturbing our lesson by barking and jumping up at the piano. Her parents also thought that this was a babysitting opportunity, allowing them time to go out and do their errands.

My initial thought was how fortunate I had been to have had a skilled teacher who knew what she was doing when I was four and how well-behaved I was at that age. This teaching job was quite different from my own experience of being a student. For weeks, whenever I went there to teach, I thought about quitting. No matter how hard I tried or how often I changed up the lesson plan, every lesson ended with a disaster I hadn't prepared for. Not only did she find playing the piano boring, but she also refused to listen to what I instructed. Asking her to play a few notes on one hand felt like an impossible task—like moving a mountain. *Am I wasting my time here?*

I ended up quitting the job after all. In the last lesson, I cried in front of my five-year-old student, lamenting, "What do you want me to do? 'Cause I really don't know what to do."

I felt embarrassed and helpless.

Teaching piano is difficult . . .

Fast-forward to years later. Fortunately, I didn't give up teaching the piano. On the contrary, I have come to enjoy it very much. Unlike performing, teaching fascinates me in the way that I draw out music from someone else. Finding the unique beauty in a person and drawing it out of them through music is a creative process. Throughout my school years as a piano major, I continually taught piano on the side, and during my doctoral studies, I even taught undergraduate group piano classes as a teaching assistant.

Although I haven't been made to cry in front of my students as I did with that first one, I often ask myself, *If I could go back in time with that five-year-old student in Korea, would I know how to do what I do now?*

This question actually led me to return to school to get another master's degree in piano pedagogy and to learn how to teach piano properly. I couldn't believe I was going back to school, even after a rigorous doctoral program in piano performance at Indiana University. *Haven't I had enough schooling already?* Yet I knew I had to find an answer to the doubt I had in myself as a teacher.

In my audition interview, the advisor asked me, "What do you think your weakness is as a piano teacher?"

I said, "A very young beginner. Imagining teaching a group of four-year-olds terrifies me!"

I didn't realize that the answer would lead me to become a certified teacher for the early childhood music program *Musikgarten*, which I went through officially in Chicago. For the following four years, I taught music to kindergarten and first-grade students every Friday in public elementary schools in Indianapolis—yes, a group of them at the same time! Though challenging, I cherished every minute of this experience, jumping and dancing with them with music and happily singing a song, hand in hand, with those kids, who were bundles of joy.

After performing, teaching the piano is one of my biggest passions. I can picture myself teaching piano as late as I am able to as a part of my life. If my health allows, I might even be teaching piano in my nineties (fingers crossed).

Now, I am no longer scared of teaching young beginners or a group of small kids. However, having had experiences over the last two decades of teaching in almost every possible setting, from an early childhood music program to undergraduate piano majors, I've discovered that there are two specific groups of students whom I most enjoy teaching: passionate adult students and intermediate or advanced late teenagers. I finally realized that whenever I teach a young beginner, I have to expend more energy than I gain, regardless of my skills as a teacher.

The piano has been a place to comfort my soul, especially during my teens, right after my parents' divorce. Taking piano lessons and practicing piano were my sanctuaries to replenish my energy and heal. Throughout my life, using the piano as a source of growth has been a recurring theme. If I were doing good focused work while practicing piano, it meant that my mind was on the right track to becoming calm. Piano and life have long been inseparable for me. That is why, as a teacher, I am also drawn to these two groups of students.

Adult students bring a whole different challenge into our lessons: questions about life and personal struggles. Yet these students enjoy creating music as an oasis in their lives. They become kids on a musical playground. I get to help them with the unique challenge of playing the piano as an adult, which is different for young beginners. Additionally, mentoring teenagers is rewarding for me as I am able to help guide their lives with music, as I experienced in my youth. Not to mention I enjoy teaching advanced repertoires. Those students tackle such music without qualms or fear.

I am proudest of myself in my journey of teaching piano because I kept pushing toward the limit of what I was afraid of. Doing exactly what I didn't want to face has taught me much about myself—what I love doing and how to navigate my life confidently.

Do you have anything that you are afraid of? How did you get over the fear?

I encourage you to take a chance and work toward it directly. Taking those uncomfortable steps might be the best thing you can do for your future self and may unlock a new discovery within you.

Concert Corner

Variations on "Ah vous dirai-je, Maman," K. 265
by Wolfgang Amadeus Mozart

Play the Piano by Jin Young Park

9.

What Driving Taught Me About Life

In 2003, when I arrived in Bloomington, Indiana, from Korea, one of the first things I did was buy a used car—a beat-up white Dodge Neon for $2,000. I knew nothing about buying cars, so I picked something randomly from Craigslist that was within my budget. I just needed it to drive through town for groceries, because I could easily walk to campus from my apartment.

A minor problem was that I had never driven before. Although I had gotten a driver's license years before in Korea, the test involved driving in small, confined areas on roads that simulated actual roads. It was basically like passing a test after successfully driving a bumper car at an amusement park. I exchanged that Korean license for a valid international permit before I came to the United States, so I could drive legally. That is why I bought a car right away. I know: It was crazy!

I thought the streets in Bloomington were so spacious and had so few cars compared with Korea that it looked doable. *I just need to know where my accelerator is to go forward and how to stop the car, right? Easy enough!* I held up my closed fist to the sky, pretending I could do it, while ignoring a little doubt underneath.

For the next few weeks, things went well. Driving through local streets was no different from the test I had taken in Korea. I stayed between the lines, looked both ways when I turned, and checked the rearview mirror to see who was behind me. Luckily, there was no need to parallel park in Bloomington, so I avoided that at all costs. I felt like I had finally become an adult who knew what she was doing.

You could tell that the car was old. Some of the white paint on the exterior had been removed, and the windows were often stuck, even when yanking hard on the manual window handle. However, unless it was freezing outside, it didn't bother me. In fact, I felt like a movie star when I drove with the windows down, the breeze on my face, and my favorite music on.

A couple of times, I came across challenges. I vividly remember waiting for the traffic light to change, and another car was coming from the opposite direction, right at me. I was as startled as the other driver. *What is going on?* As the other driver slowed his car down to a stop in the middle of the intersection, he pointed to a sign that said, "One Way." I was clearly going the wrong way—practically waiting for someone to crash into me at any moment. Thankfully, there wasn't an accident. He seemed to take it with a sense of humor. *Thank you, I thought.* I let out a huge sigh of relief and made a mental note to be more careful about noticing those one-way signs. They were everywhere once I started looking for them.

The real test, however, was driving at night. Something about driving in the dark without many street lights made everything harder: watching for other cars, people, or deer; turning; or even seeing the road signs or the stripes on the road.

One evening, I was driving home from a grocery store around 9 p.m. I held the steering wheel tightly to feel safer. Then, a police car turned on its light and siren right behind me. I looked in the rearview mirror, confused. *Is he coming after me? What did I do wrong? I was driving only 20 miles per hour, way under the speed limit of 35. Maybe I was driving* too slow? *Could that be a problem?* A million thoughts came to me as I pulled the car to the side.

The police officer slowly approached and asked me to roll down the window. "Is it hard for you to drive?" he said.

I was surprised to hear that question and thought, *How did he know?* I gave him a little smile and said, "Sometimes . . ."

Without much change in his dry expression, he bluntly said, "Turn on your headlights. It's better that way."

That was a big aha moment for me, except I didn't know where the light switch was. I mean . . . I had never used it since I started driving. I had to ask the officer where that switch was, and he helped me turn on the lights. I was genuinely happy with the discovery—and suddenly, boom! Lights in front of the car were shining on the road ahead. "Ah! That *is* better!"

The officer warned me that he would have to give me a ticket the next time I forgot, shook his head, and left. He must have thought I was crazy, but I was just glad to have learned some important information about driving at night.

I can proudly report that, since that night, I have never been pulled over by the police in over two decades. I'm not sure if I can say I am a skilled driver, but I like driving a stick shift when I have the option, and I am a careful and patient driver who doesn't take risks on the road.

When I come across crazy drivers, I think about myself in those earlier times. Maybe that is why I don't have road rage. I give the person in front of me the benefit of the doubt and drive preventively to avoid accidents whenever possible.

One of the life lessons I learned from driving a car is to interpret other drivers' unreasonable behavior as being caused by an emergency or some other valid reason rather than my first thought being that they are neglectful or reckless.

My favorite mindset shift was realizing that I would do the same as others if I were in their situation. If someone cuts me off in traffic, I think they're probably late for work. If I see someone making wrong decisions in life, I usually think that I might do the same if I were living their life with the same childhood, parents, and experiences.

Maybe that is not always true; they might indeed be reckless. Ultimately, however, it doesn't matter to me what their truth is. What matters is that I am more peaceful and compassionate toward others by not allowing negative assumptions into my mind.

The next time someone cuts you off in traffic, please give them the benefit of the doubt rather than becoming instantly irritated. My younger clumsy beginner-driver self will thank you for that generosity.

Concert Corner

Impromptu in E-flat Major, Op. 90, No. 2, D. 899 by Franz Schubert

Oh! Voyage by Van ▶

10. I Appreciate You For . . .

Because I grew up in Korea, Thanksgiving has been a new holiday for me. I have to admit that I am still puzzled by the National Thanksgiving Turkey Presentation, a ceremony that takes place at the White House and consists of the president pardoning one turkey. What value does it add? Equally, the Black Friday madness after the holiday took time for me to get used to, and I avoided the crowds at all costs.

In Korea, we have a similar autumn holiday, a celebration of the harvest called Chu-Seok. As a traditionally agricultural country, Korea values celebrating and giving thanks for new crops and wishing for a good upcoming year. I explained to Mom that Thanksgiving in the United States is like Chu-Seok in Korea, when families gather with their extended members and enjoy a feast together.

I love the word *thanksgiving* and the concept behind this beautiful holiday. Having a day of giving thanks allows us time to stop and count our blessings.

On our three-year anniversary, my boyfriend and I shared the qualities of each other that we most appreciated. During our sunset walk, we took turns elaborating on these qualities and when we saw them demonstrated. I smiled widely like a little kid and said, "Tell me more, please!" After hours of this sweet conversation, we both felt loved and appreciated. Because words of affirmation are one of my primary love languages, I thrived on this.

Coincidentally, I recently discovered the wonderful work of Dr. John Gottman about relationships and communication among people. One of the exercises that he suggested from his research is known as "I Appreciate . . ." He suggests thinking of someone in your life to whom you wish to express appreciation. First, think of three great qualities in that person, and then describe a time when the person displayed these qualities.

For example, if the characteristic is "cheerful," you might say, "One memorable occasion when you displayed your cheerful nature was during a family gathering. Despite challenging circumstances, you managed to keep the atmosphere light and joyful, making everyone feel relaxed and happy."

Last week, I practiced this with my friends. I loved the specific instructions on expressing yourself to someone in your life and suggesting actionable steps. I found it interesting that writing these qualities alone was not difficult, but delivering the message and sharing it with the person required a bit of bravery. If this is out of character for you, initiating it would be even more complicated. The delivery form, however, can vary. It could be an email, a conversation, a handwritten thank-you card, a voice memo, or a good old simple text, like we do every day.

Imagine that one of your best friends texted you, saying the following: "I was just doing some journaling, and I wanted to say that I really appreciate these three qualities about you: You are thoughtful, caring, and very generous. I will share more when we meet, but I really wanted to share this with you now, because I appreciate having you in my life!"

How would you feel about receiving or giving this message?

Having said that, I want to thank all of you for being on the other side of this essay and being a part of my creative endeavors in music and life. Your appreciation of what I do fuels me to keep moving forward and adds meaning to my life. Thank you.

Now, it is your turn. Who would you like to express your gratitude to? I challenge you to take Dr. John Gottman's suggestion and try at least one "I Appreciate . . ." exercise with someone you care about. Take note of how you feel afterward or how you made that person feel. Sometimes, just making a tiny gesture creates a big ripple effect.

Concert Corner

"Wedding Day at Troldhaugen," Op. 65, No. 6 by Edvard Grieg

◀ *In Reflection's Stillness, Always Found*
by Shin Jinho

"Adventures are the best way to learn. I love places that make you realize how tiny you and your problems are. At the end of the day, your feet should be dirty, your hair messy, and your eyes sparkling."

—UNKNOWN

THE SECOND MOVEMENT:

Allegro con brio

11.

Feel the Fear . . . and Do It Anyway

Last week, I had a summer vacation in Big Sur, California, for my birthday. Swimming in the state park creeks brought back cherished memories of jumping in clean, fresh water in Korea when I was young. Just like my childhood memory, I swam in the fresh water like a kid until I couldn't possibly do it anymore. I laughed like a kid. I played like there was nothing else that existed in the world. The swimming hole was surrounded by trees and birds singing their songs. How refreshing it was!

During this visit, I also immersed myself in the book *Feel the Fear . . . and Do It Anyway* by Susan Jeffers. This book was recommended for its performance anxiety tips, which were helpful for my students and myself. The moment I read the title, I knew I would love the book. On the surface, the book had nothing to do with music. However, in the end, this conversation about life was inevitably related to music-making and being vulnerable on a performance stage.

The book describes three levels of fears. Level 1 fears are divided into those that happen to us, such as aging, becoming disabled, losing a loved one, illness, or natural disasters. The second group of level 1 fears are those requiring action, such as making decisions, changing a career, and ending or beginning a relationship.

Then, there are the level 2 fears, which are not situation oriented but involve the ego, such as rejection, shame, failure, loss of image, disapproval, and disappointment. These have to do with inner states of mind rather than exterior situations. They reflect our sense of self and our ability to handle this world. If we fear rejection, this fear will affect almost every area of our lives. So we begin to protect ourselves and, as a result, greatly limit ourselves.

The level 3 fears get down to the nitty-gritty of the issue: the biggest fear of all. That is the fear of "I can't handle it!" Apparently, at the bottom of every one of our fears is simply the fear that we can't handle whatever life may bring us.

Level 1 fear translates to level 3 in these examples:

> I can't handle illness.
>
> I can't handle losing my money.
>
> I can't handle losing my partner.
>
> I can't handle getting old.

Or level 2 fear translates to level 3 like this:

I can't handle being rejected.

I can't handle failure.

I can't handle being humiliated.

The author says that the level 3 fear of "I can't handle it!" is the basis of all other fears. She asks, "If you knew you could handle anything that came your way, what would you possibly have to fear?"

Nothing!

All you have to do to diminish your fear is to develop more trust in your ability to handle whatever comes your way!

The biggest takeaway from the book for me was this reminder: *I can handle anything that comes my way. I trust that I will figure it out.*

Whenever there is a big performance coming up, I always tell myself this: *All I have to do is to be in the present moment. I will let the music carry me.*

Then, I also remind myself that I can always pick myself up from whatever mistake may occur. Mistakes onstage are not within my control. I can't expect that I will perform with every-note perfection. However, I can control how I handle it; I will get back up and continue making music no matter what situation I might be in.

This mindset has always given me tremendous strength as I navigate being vulnerable every time I take both the musical and life stage and perform.

I'll be able to handle it.

There are four truths about fear the author shares:

- **Truth 1:** The fear will never go away as long as I continue to grow.
- **Truth 2:** The only way to get rid of the fear of doing something is to go out and do it.
- **Truth 3:** The only way to feel better about myself is to go out and do it.
- **Truth 4:** Not only am I going to experience fear whenever I'm on unfamiliar territory, but so is everyone else.

Are you afraid of doing something? Do you feel hesitant to take that next step?

Welcome the fear.

It's part of being human.

Let's feel the fear . . . and do it anyway.

Concert Corner

Gymnopédie No. 1 by Erik Satie

Beyond the Now, My Eyes Must Reach by Shin Jinho

12.

Lessons Learned from My Surfing Adventure

Last week, I spent a week in Oahu, Hawaii, giving a workshop for music teachers and a master class to talented young musicians at the Masaki School of Music. I was pleasantly surprised by the students' high level of musicianship in this paradise.

My relationship with Nancy Masaki, the school's director and also a cellist at the Hawaii Symphony Orchestra, started about three years ago, when I needed a space to practice during my vacation. She has graciously allowed me to practice there ever since. I can relax better during vacation if I can access a piano, even if just for a little bit. Because of this secured spot to practice, Oahu has been my go-to spot to decompress and take a break.

That was also the first time I had seen beautiful Waikiki Beach full of surfers, from beginners to advanced. Living in San Diego as I do, I see surfing everywhere. But I never thought of trying it.

Waikiki was different. Something about that wide-open blue water with Diamond Head as the backdrop made everything, even surfing, seem inviting and doable.

I told my boyfriend that I would try surfing the following day for the first time. As an avid surfer, he welcomed the idea and perhaps internally shouted, *Yes!* He had gently nudged the idea of surfing a couple of times, but my answer was always firm: No.

Looking at the clock right before my first surf, it said 3 a.m. I had been watching dozens of "How to Surf" YouTube videos all night, trying different pop-up techniques on the yoga mat. By sunrise, I felt ready. Like an Olympian before a match, I could imagine myself gliding down the ocean like a pro from those videos.

My boyfriend showed me how to put a leash around my ankle, and he started to paddle out without much explanation. I hurried back and followed him. Though I had no surfing experience, I was a good swimmer. *Just swim with a board on my belly. Not a big deal, right?* The place he took me was a surf break called Pops, which took at least twenty minutes for us to paddle out to. It felt long, but I didn't say anything. Later, I learned that Pops is an unusual surf break, and to reach it, one must paddle a long distance from the shore. It felt like I was swimming across a football stadium twice, back and forth.

When we finally arrived, three or four locals were waiting for the waves at the break. Another thing I didn't realize was that it was a six- to eight-foot wave day. To give some perspective, I consider anything bigger than four feet too big for me, knowing what that feels like now. Surely, that day, the waves looked giant, making me paddle even more outside to feel safer. As I was the farthest out in the lineup, one local finally shouted to me, "It is *your* turn!" noticing that I had been waiting for a while, passing good waves back to them.

Finally, I paddled close to one of them and announced with a smile, "Hi! This is my first day of surfing! I'm so happy to be here today!"

I still vividly remember the locals' facial expressions at that moment, looking perplexed and confused. One of them told me nicely that I was in the wrong spot as a first-time surfer and asked how in the world I could paddle out this far as a beginner.

Finally, my boyfriend suggested going to a beginner-friendly spot. I think that all along, he knew I was in the wrong place, but he probably needed to take a couple of big waves before babysitting me. Just like I had envisioned, one wave approached from far away. I started to paddle to catch it, and there I was, riding my first wave ever on my belly. I couldn't pop up that day, but I caught seven unbroken green waves on my belly, screaming like a little kid every time.

When I came back to San Diego, I announced that I would give surfing a solid six months with total effort. Knowing how challenging this sport might be, anything under six months didn't seem right. After purchasing my first board, I faced the first challenge. I didn't have a surf rack on my little Fiat car. I found out that there was no way I could install a surf rack on this particular car model. That was when I drove to a used-car dealer and switched my car to a Mini Cooper. It's a similar small car, but now with a surf rack. The dealer asked if there was anything in particular I was looking for, and I said, "I just need a surf rack."

I thought everything would be smooth sailing from there, except it wasn't. Apparently, the real test hadn't started yet. The following month, I was in agony of being unable to pop up on the board no matter what I tried. Almost toward the end of that first month, I started to think I was not a person who could surf, period. In the big picture, yes, a month is not long, but it felt like an eternity. Every time when I came back from "surfing"—which wasn't surfing at all because I was just floating in the water—I felt stupid, uncoordinated, intimidated, frustrated, and, mostly, sad. Popping up seemed an impossible task no matter what I tried. *If I can't stand on the board, it is* not *surfing. It is called boogie boarding . . .*

One beautiful morning, when I still hadn't succeeded in my pop-up, my surfing coach, a female champion surfer named Michelle Bautista Layton, told me, "Today, you will pop up on the board no matter what." She was holding a shiny wooden board in her arms. Apparently, what she brought that day for me was a family treasure: an eleven-foot balsa board. Balsa is a lightweight wood that makes a board buoyant and able to glide easily. Such boards tend to be heavy and often pricey, too. She said she was late that morning because it took longer than she thought to remove the board from its place as a wall decoration.

I didn't know how valuable the thing was, but I could tell it had a particular look, as if it had a spirit. Just like a piano made out of wood, something about a board made of wood was different to touch, hold, and paddle. It had its own way of existing in the water. When the first good wave was approaching, Michelle said, "Go ahead, paddle, and pop up!"

The next few seconds were vague, as when I woke up from those seconds, I was flying on the water with the beautiful balsa board under my feet. I looked to the left, where I wanted to go, and the board led the way, making a smooth turn. Just like that, I got to pop up and surf for the first time. Michelle was ecstatic, screaming behind me and praising me for turning the board in the first pop-up.

All I can say is that I had been surfing in my mind for so long that my body knew what to do once I got up.

The rest is history.

No, I am not good at surfing, but I am happy to report that I can pop up and ride a wave. I like a gentle two- to three-foot wave at sunrise in mild weather.

I'm sure I look uncool in the water because I cover myself from head to toe, literally, except my eyes. Or, to look at it positively, I look like a ninja.

After six months of giving surf a full trial, I finally realized that there were a couple missing pieces in my life that surfing was teaching me—a connection with nature and being a beginner at something all over again.

Last week in Oahu, I surfed almost every morning. Many beginners were trying this sport for the first time and catching their first waves. Seeing them from a distance made me realize how far I've come and how grateful I am to have surfing in my life.

Concert Corner

"Reflets dans l'eau" ("Reflections in the Water")
from *Images, Book 1* by Claude Debussy

Riding the Keys, Riding the Waves by Jack Soren

SOREN

13.

The Power of Unlearning

I used to go to bookstores all the time. A memory of drinking hot chocolate with whipped cream on top (which I haven't had for decades) at a coffee shop inside the Barnes & Noble bookstore in Bloomington, Indiana, is a nostalgic scene for me. Not to mention, in my vivid recollection, the view outside the window was often covered in snow. I would grab a stack of new books that piqued my interest and skim through them while sipping a hot chocolate. It was always my solo downtime activity that I looked forward to whenever I needed mental space.

Sadly, nowadays, my book purchases are mostly made online. Every transaction is quick and efficient. Although I doubt that I can ever go back to buying books in a bookstore regularly, still,

I miss browsing new books in the aisle—making that random discovery. For a change, I would walk to a category I didn't usually go to. Holding the new book close to my nose, I would sniff it like some fancy perfume. I would read them through for hours. I don't recall buying those stacks of books back then, as I couldn't justify the price in my small budget. Yet I still felt it was just as much fun.

Ironically, nowadays, one of the last bookstores I still regularly visit is at the airport—five minutes before boarding, ten minutes before transferring to another gate. Unlike in my student years, I now have little time for browsing. Rather, I glance quickly, get whatever seems interesting on first impression, and run to my destination, clutching a new book.

That happened a couple of weeks ago at the San Diego airport. I grabbed a copy of *Think Again* by Adam Grant. Knowing the author fairly well from his other amazing books, such as *Originals* and *Give and Take*, I knew it would be good. However, I was surprised by how insightful this book was! I let out an audible "Wow . . ." multiple times on that plane ride. I could feel a curiosity from the passenger beside me with his side glance. With a record decision time (perhaps it took thirty seconds) to make the purchase, this book surely delivered much more than my expectations.

Adam Grant writes, "When people reflect on what it takes to be mentally fit, the first idea that comes to mind is usually intelligence. The smarter you are, the more complex the problems you can solve—and the faster you can solve them. Intelligence is traditionally viewed as the ability to think and learn. Yet, in a turbulent world, there's another set of cognitive skills that might matter more: the ability to rethink and unlearn."

The book is about the value of rethinking. It is an invitation to let go of knowledge and opinions that no longer serve you well and to anchor your sense of self in flexibility rather than consistency. With COVID-19, we all had a huge nudge of rethinking and unlearning. What had worked in the past didn't work anymore. For a while, we held on to the assumption that it wouldn't affect our lives to the degree that it did and then were forced to reprogram our thinking on what to do about it.

According to Grant's book, people often fall into the habit of thinking in three different modes. These are: 1. preacher (I am right.); 2. prosecutor (They are wrong!); or 3. politician (We are right! They are wrong.).

Grant's favorite bias is "I'm not biased," in which people believe they're more objective than others. It turns out that smart people are more likely to fall into this trap. The brighter you are, the harder it can be to see your own limitations. Being good at thinking can make you worse at rethinking. Isn't that interesting?

The author suggests that while there are situations in which it might make sense to preach, prosecute, and politick, we can all benefit by more often making the effort to think like a scientist. Being a scientist is not just a profession but a frame of mind, searching for the truth: We run experiments to test hypotheses and discover knowledge. The purpose of learning isn't to affirm our beliefs; it's to evolve our beliefs.

He also writes, "We don't start with answers or solutions; we lead with questions and puzzles. We don't preach from intuition; we teach from evidence. We don't just have healthy skepticism about other people's arguments; we dare to disagree with our own arguments. It means being actively open-minded. It requires searching for reasons we might be wrong—not for reasons we must be right—and revising our views based on what we learn."

Here are three more insights from the book that made me think:

1. Embrace the joy of being wrong. Whenever you realize that you made a mistake, that is a sign that you have just discovered something new. How exciting! It helps you focus less on proving yourself—and more on improving yourself.
2. Don't shy away from constructive conflict. I've learned that disagreements don't have to be disagreeable. Don't take it personally; rather, approach what is probably a task conflict as a debate. If this debate were televised, how would you support your arguments, and what kind of evidence would you use? A debate is like a dance, not a war. Admitting the other person's views doesn't make you weaker but shows your willingness to rethink and be flexible, which motivates others to consider their views as well. It's helpful to have cheerleaders encouraging you in your life, but you also need people who can challenge you and invite you to rethink with freedom of choice and love.

3. Question how rather than why. When people have a strong view of something, they often attach the view to their identity, creating a wall of not listening. Instead of asking why they hold that view, ask how they could make their views reality. The same applies when we ask ourselves questions. Make a habit of asking how you formed an opinion in the first place and what evidence would make you change your mind.

Whenever I have new project ideas, whether for the next album, courses to teach, or a concert format change, I build strong reasoning around my initial thoughts. I protect my ideas on why something should work a certain way. Since I spent many hours developing a new concept, I feel protective of it—so much so that I often feel other people's opinions are like an attack on my artistic endeavor. However, the more I try to listen to what others have to say in the process, the better the outcome. In the end, by listening to varied ideas, I can see my blind spots and then make a better choice.

You would be surprised by how many drafts and edits I go through before I have a final project realized: months, if not years, of changing and rearranging. As tedious and demanding as these ever-changing stages can be, I learned to enjoy listening to different perspectives and having fun accepting other ideas into my thinking playground. I've always come out grateful for my mind's flexibility to listen to another perspective.

When was the last time you had to rethink and change your point of view?

Research suggests that the more frequently we make fun of ourselves, the happier we tend to be. Instead of beating ourselves up about our mistakes, we can turn some of our past misconceptions into sources of present amusement.

What Brené Brown said in a review of Grant's book resonates with me: "Yes, learning requires focus. But unlearning and relearning require much more—it requires choosing courage over comfort. This helps us build the intellectual and emotional muscle that we need to stay curious enough about the world to actually change it. I've never felt so hopeful about what I don't know."

Angry Charlie by Selynn Lee

14.

The Impossible Task

The years from 2011 to 2016 were the hardest time of my life. Despite the honor of becoming Dr. Kim with a doctoral degree in piano performance from one of the most reputable music schools—Indiana University—my life was upside down.

I went through a difficult and unexpected divorce because of my ex-husband's drug addiction. Not only did I lose the person I loved, but the well-being of our close circle of family and friends has never been the same since. From this experience, I finally opened my eyes to the dark reality of drug addiction and its extreme difficulties.

When I relocated to the West Coast to a promising academic position at a state university, I was full of hope that I could become a professor, which quickly broke into pieces after I made the brave move from the Midwest. I did not have an agent at the time or any concert engagements lined up. My hope of playing concerts internationally was far from reality. I was jobless and didn't know anyone. All of my family members lived in Korea. I was alone. In every corner, all I saw was darkness—I was in survival mode as I crawled through this dark tunnel.

Dreaming something for the future was unthinkable at the time. I considered it a success if I made it through the entire day without breaking down.

I remember music being my only solace, as it had always been. I kept practicing piano to reconnect with myself and the universe. At least in that artistic realm, I was safe and free.

Living in San Diego since 2015 has been a blessing to my healing process. Even in the darkest moments, that Southern California sunshine always came through to remind me that all is well. I realized that I could still laugh at silly jokes, foods still tasted great, and the ocean breeze felt pleasant on my skin.

And just like that, I was gradually developing a muscle to not only survive but to thrive in this life.

That was when I decided to embark on an idea for my first album, *10 More Minutes*. It began through a Kickstarter crowd-funding project with a pledge goal of $30,000. I wanted to create an album that captured that special feeling of wanting just ten more minutes of whatever it is that gives you pure bliss. I recorded a selection of pieces that reminded me of a warm hug from a dear friend when you really need one.

I said to myself, *People will love it! I can share my oasis with the world.*

In times of despair, I found a glimmer of hope that I could get back up again.

Even though I was skeptical of the project's success, I was willing to bet on myself. I knew going into it that there was no loss in this attempt. I thought to myself, *If I am able to get funded, I will fulfill my dream of creating and sharing my first album with the world. If I am unable to get funded, I will learn from it and gain momentum to move forward.*

Asking for donations from friends and strangers was a humbling experience. I had to practice delivering the same sentences over and over again, before even mentioning the project funding. Accepting a no as an answer was not an issue for me because I didn't take it personally. I, however, felt terrible for those who might have felt guilty for saying no. I did not like that I might be putting them in an awkward position.

Somehow, a miracle occurred.

Donations started to roll in one by one: $10 here, $20 there, $1,000 sometimes . . . or more.

More people were enthusiastic about the project than I initially thought.

They said, "I can't wait to listen to the album. Go for it!" "I love your music. I hope your dream comes true." "Thank you for creating this music for us." "We love you, Jeeyoon!" "What a great idea!" "Cheering for you!"

Every dollar donated to the project had a message of encouragement attached.

I felt supported, encouraged, lifted, and surrounded by love.

After completing the crowdfunding campaign, I flew to New York to record the album. I shared every step of the progress with my supporters—my whereabouts, the look of my cover shots, and how far along I was with the album.

The moment the finalized album arrived at my doorstep, I shared it excitedly with my supporters and friends. They were as excited as I was, if not more. The 2016 album release of *10 More Minutes* was a celebration that I shared with the world.

"We did it together!"

Yes, I was the one who played the piano and recorded the album, but it would not have come to fruition without the wind in my sails created by all those wonderful supporters. I was merely playing my role in a much larger endeavor.

I was a messenger of music.

That was it. That was how I found my mission.

The moment this album became a reality, I was reborn as an artist.

In every new project, concert, and album, I have that mission in mind: *How can I serve? How can I share more? How can I be more of a messenger of music so that people can receive its healing and uplifting powers?*

Some might say that it is a story of great luck, and some might say that it is a story of triumph.

I would say that it is a story of love.

My life did not offer me a smooth red-carpet path. Jagged rocks and dusty roads trained me to become who I am today—the Jeeyoon whom you know. I am forever grateful for the wisdom I have gained from my life's darkest valleys.

Whenever I face a new challenge or when I feel discouraged by my own criticism, I need to hear my story again. It's the journey that I am currently on—a reminder to myself of all the mountains that I have climbed, giving myself a much-needed lift.

We all have a story. It doesn't have to be enormous or earth-shattering. The truth is that we all have come far from where we began. Storyteller and author Matthew Dicks emphasizes that one must view one's life story as a journey—an adventure worthy of investment, excitement, and continuous movement forward.

Rather than looking at your life through the small lens of the immediate moment or an ominous unknown future, you must expand your view to all that came before and all that could be. Take credit for your achievements. Try to view this very day as a scene in a greater story you can tell yourself.

Please tell your story—especially to yourself.

When the story of your battles and their eventual victories are alive in your heart and mind, you will see that the next battle is nothing you can't overcome.

It was true for me.

Concert Corner

Piano Sonata No. 6 in F Major, Op. 10, No. 2 by Ludwig van Beethoven

Piano in the Window by Kaoru Yamada

15.

The Art of Fun

This week, some ideas from the book *Feel-Good Productivity* by Ali Abdaal struck a chord with me. Abdaal came across the message from a song in the musical *Mary Poppins,* which says when we make things fun—like a game—even our work becomes easier to do.

He decided to apply this idea to his own life. In a late-night burst of inspiration, he grabbed a Sharpie and a Post-it note and wrote nine simple words: *What would this look like if it were fun?* Then, one day, while tackling a boring task that he didn't want to do, he sincerely asked himself, *Could I do this differently? Could I add music or humor or get creative? What if I tackled the task with friends or promised myself a treat at the end?*

After experiencing the transformative effects of this thinking process, it has become a guiding question in his life.

Just as it took some time for Abdaal to connect deeply with the question, I had this question in my mind for several weeks: *What* would *this look like if it were fun?* Then, I realized that unconsciously, this fundamental question underlies everything I do each day, seeking a more enjoyable approach.

How can I practice this same piece of music differently today to make it more fun?

Is there a way to make this process a little more enjoyable?

I like the idea of making a conscious and ongoing effort to make tasks more fun. After all, we are naturally drawn to seeking good times in life! When I shifted from unconsciously seeking fun to making it an intentional part of every task, I found that I could seamlessly and more easily integrate the fun factor.

I always encourage my piano students to be creative in their daily practice. Sometimes, just by tweaking minor details, daily tasks can become much more enjoyable!

Here are several ideas that I've experimented with:

1. Work on computer-related work at my favorite cafe. Something about the cafe environment gives me an extra boost of energy that turns undesirable work into fun—whether it's doing taxes, composing email responses, scheduling, writing a draft, or reading a chapter of a book

that I've been putting off. Often, after a couple of hours of work, I feel a sense of accomplishment from deep work, which I find fun. I wondered why I couldn't do the same thing at home. Interestingly, and fortunately, this trick of going to a cafe always works for me.

2. Put on a piece of music while doing chores. Music in the background often gives me spring-cleaning energy.
3. Create a mini reward system. Whether it's a snack, a cup of matcha, lunch, surfing, watching YouTube, or a hot bath, I make it a reward for completing x, y, and z. By placing the reward after the task, I find it effective to tackle the work with a bit more ease.
4. Practice a performance wearing concert shoes or a special gown. This extra effort makes the whole run-through practice more vital.
5. Do tasks with friends. One of the most enjoyable activities during the COVID-19 quarantine was meeting with my students weekly on Zoom and practicing simultaneously for thirty minutes with their computer audio muted. Many commented that the thirty minutes flew by like three minutes and were fun. There are similar "study together with me" or "read a book with me" models on YouTube, in which people do things together, even virtually. Doing things together with others can be a powerful tool.

6. Impose time limits. Setting a time limit often turns a task into a game. What if I only had a fifteen-minute time block or a five-minute limit to do a task that I feel too lazy to do? I set a timer on my phone. Not only does this help me complete the task more efficiently, but it also gives me a dose of motivation to get started.

Do you have tasks you don't enjoy doing? I hope you consider reframing them to make them fun!

Concert Corner

"Golliwogg's Cakewalk" from *Children's Corner* by Claude Debussy

The First Snow by MOSLA

16.

Secrets to a Deeper Connection with Classical Music

Last week, I had the privilege of visiting local high schools in Crescent City, California, where I performed solo concerts. Presenters often arrange for artists to visit schools during their stays, giving the musicians more direct opportunities to engage with the community before the concert. I love these connections, because I get to talk about the beauty of classical music and how to connect with it better outside the concert context.

Making my way through students' bustling hallway traffic between classes is always a fresh experience. In Korea, we stay in one classroom for the entire school year (in fact, the same assigned desk), and different teachers come to us. As I walked into a classroom full of high school students, some looked curious and happy to face someone new, and others looked indifferent and unsure about the whole thing.

Over the years, I've realized that I've lived a rather unusual life as far as classical music is concerned. As the graduate of an art high school in Korea, I majored in piano as a young teenager. Then, getting a higher education degree and becoming a doctor of musical arts (DMA) in piano performance put me in academia until my late twenties, surrounded by fellow classical music nerds for almost all my life. I didn't have to explain the beauty of classical music to them. We were just fellow fanatics who loved to share and talk about it.

Then, I hit a big reality check after leaving the school once I started to perform in front of an actual audience. I realized that the general public needs more context when encountering classical music. After all, the piano is no longer a center of entertainment in their living rooms, and people are moving away from classical music traditions. The good news is that once I gave my listeners a better context, almost everyone found their way to classical music and loved it. I saw that not only did they become fans of classical music once given the right context and setting, but they also became fellow lifelong supporters of what I do: act as an ambassador of classical music.

In that California classroom, I asked how many of the students had been to a classical concert in the past. Only a handful raised their hands shyly. I assume you are reading this because you have had some exposure to classical music and already love it. But setting that assumption aside, I want to offer the same secrets that I offered to those high school students on how to connect more deeply with this music that I love.

Here are six tips that I would like to offer you to try to connect more deeply with classical music:

1. **Choose a medium.** There are so many instrumentation possibilities in classical music. Choose one or two instrumentations, such as string quartet, piano, piano trio, flute, cello, baritone, etc., and dig deeper. The more familiar you become with a specific instrumentation, the more you will feel at home when you listen to it as an introduction.
2. **Be a superfan of several classical musicians.** There are many classical music rock stars in this world. Don't blindly follow what others follow, but find with whom you can connect and be a superfan; listen to their albums, go to their live concerts, follow their social media, and find ways to stay connected with them through their YouTube appearances or newsletters. Yes, I do follow others myself! Among them are pianist Maria João Pires and conductor Kirill Petrenko, whose concert I hope to attend in the future.
3. **Choose one piece of classical music you connect with, and listen to many different versions.** Interestingly, classical music is ironic in that you don't have to know anything to appreciate it, but your appreciation surely deepens the

more intimately you know the piece. I've never met anyone who said, "Oh, I know that piece so well, so I don't have to go to the concert to listen to it again." The more you love a piece, the more eagerly you want to listen to that piece over and over again. This also leads one to be curious about how other artists would interpret it.

4. **Go to live performances.** Nothing beats a live performance, period. Yes, I do understand the convenience of YouTube and other digital mediums, and I am thankful for those. However, unless you live on a rural mountain at some far end of the earth, I bet you can find some live classical concerts somewhere. This is about a human connection—one human creates art, and another human receives it. Go and experience it for yourself. Then, do it again and again. Start small. At the beginning, an intimate house concert might have a better impact than a big hall for orchestra. Listen to the repertoire before the concert to equip yourself, turn off the phone, and allow yourself to fully receive the gift of music for an hour.

5. **Be an active listener.** That means you need to participate in the music. Can you think of some image or story or your experience while you listen? What would the composer have been thinking, doing, or feeling when he or she wrote? Can you connect with the performer? Tap into any emotions that arise in you, and follow them with the music. Don't be

afraid to go off on your own thoughts. That is a sign that your heart is responding to that music.

6. **Learn an instrument.** This is the hardest way to do it, but it is the surest way to guarantee you will become a classical music fan. Once you taste creating magic in music yourself, you can never reverse it. You will be hooked on the sound of this music for life.

Many of those high school students I met came to the concert. They wrote letters and talked to me afterward, thanking me for sharing my passion with them and for the inspiration. Maybe I didn't change the world, but I do believe that the power of classical music indeed touched the hearts of some people in the audience in meaningful ways—which is, to me, changing the world.

Under Starry Sky by Shin Jinho

17.

A Timeless Lesson from David

Almost fifteen years ago, on a humid, sunny afternoon in Indiana, I sat in an office with my mentor, David Bremer. I was relieved that the sounds of crickets from outside covered the sound of my crying and our conversation, as if the world could hear us otherwise.

I lamented, "I worked too hard to deserve this disaster in my life. Why did it happen to me?"

David just glanced at me and handed me a tissue. "Well," he responded, "you know what I am gonna say, don't you? Are you asking yourself a 'why' question or 'what to do now'? Asking why always points your perspective to the past, things that have already happened, or something you can't control. When you truly ask what to do at this moment from the thing that has already happened, you will gain a sense of strength and know the answer that is already within you. Don't be a baby. Grow up and learn."

Ouch. I knew better than to expect warm fuzzies from him . . .

At the same time, I found myself nodding at his comments and wiping my tears. I had to admit that he did have a point. I was looking at things in my past that were out of my control—not things I could do now within my control.

David was my mentor from when I came to the United States in my early twenties until he passed away seven years ago from cancer. I miss him greatly still. I wish I could run to him whenever I want more clarity in my life. Yet I always hear his voice and am still learning from and processing the essence of his life lessons.

He had a peculiar sense of dry humor and the deep intellect and wisdom of a true peacemaker. Unless you got to know him, people often considered him a cold personality for his bluntness in telling the truth. Yet all my memories of him are about him teaching me how to love. The truth hurts sometimes, and people certainly don't like to face it, especially when it is revealed by someone else.

Despite all that, people always flocked to him to ask for help whenever they were in trouble. People knew they needed to hear his perspective and wisdom, because it always pointed in the right direction. I was surely one of them—a repeat guest who always trailed some drama. I knew that he cared deeply about me, as I did for him.

Years later, accompanying me to the airport, where I was flying to Korea for the summer, David handed me a book and said,

"Now, you are finally ready to read this book. Read it, and follow the principles it contains. You will be fine, young lady. And you're welcome!" He gave me a smile and a wink.

I looked down at the book in my hand. It was a tiny pocket-size volume titled *The Four Agreements* by Don Miguel Ruiz.

On the plane to Korea, reading the book thoroughly with a sense of awe, I understood why I might not have been ready for it a decade earlier, but now I was. Indeed, the book changed my life.

I hope you can read it at some point if the timing of your life is right for this book. I believe the author will better explain why these four agreements are crucial to our freedom than I can here on the page.

The second agreement of his four messages is, "Don't take anything personally." Nothing others do is because of what we do. What others say and do is a projection of their own reality, their own dreams. When we are immune to the opinions and actions of others, we are no longer the victims of needless suffering.

The author says:

> "It is not important to me what you think about me, and I don't take what you think personally. I don't take it personally when people say, 'Miguel, you are the best.' And I don't take it personally when they say, 'Miguel, you are the worst.' I know what I am. I don't have the need to be accepted. Whatever you think, whatever you feel, it is the way you see the world."

"Wherever you go, you will find people lying to you, and as your awareness grows, you will notice that you also lie to yourself. Do not expect people to tell you the truth because they also lie to themselves. You have to trust yourself and choose to believe or not to believe what someone says to you."

"Whatever you think, whatever you feel, I know is your problem and not my problem. It is the way you see the world. It is nothing personal, because you are dealing with yourself, not with me. You may even tell me, 'Miguel, what you are saying is hurting me.' But it is not what I am saying that is hurting you; it is that you have wounds that I touch by what I have said. You are hurting yourself."

What resonates with me the most about this agreement is that as we make a habit of not taking anything personally, we have no need to place our trust in what others do or say. To make responsible choices, we need only to trust ourselves. We are never responsible for the actions of others; we are only responsible for ourselves. When we truly understand this and refuse to take things personally, we can hardly be hurt by the careless comments or actions of others.

We are living in a difficult world. We are getting hurtful comments from naysayers about what we do or who we are all the time. The other day, I saw a negative comment on one of my blogs. It is not my first time seeing negative words online about what I do, but sometimes, it can get to me. Without reacting to it emotionally, I asked myself these five questions:

1. How much does this person know about the field?
2. How much does this person know about me?
3. Is this person's comment for my growth or the expression of their ego?
4. Is this coming from the heart of love?
5. Do I take it personally?

The answer was clear. I erased the comment, blocked the person from the website, and moved on with my day.

We can always say yes, or we can say no. It is always our choice. The key here is to follow our hearts without guilt or self-judgment. Life is hard enough without the additional weight of negativity from others.

Whatever people do, feel, think, or say, don't take it personally. Don't take *anything* personally.

Maybe this message will free you up from the things you allow yourself to suffer, just as I have needed a reminder over and over again.

"October: Autumn Song" from *The Seasons*, Op. 37a by Pyotr Ilyich Tchaikovsky

Where Festivities Bloom by Shin Jinho

18.

Why the Small Things Matter

Recently, a friend of mine undertook a huge expensive bathroom renovation. I asked her how it turned out, and she said everything went smoothly except that the color of one tile was off and didn't match the others perfectly; there was only a slight difference, but it was a mistake. The difference isn't so obvious as to be noticeable at first glance. Still, since she sits down at the toilet and stares at the wall every day, it bothers her greatly every time.

Urgh, I know that feeling . . .

She said that maybe, with time, the odd tile would become like a piece of wall art, as if it were meant to be.

I've been wanting to get a custom surfboard painted in an eggplant purple color. To ensure that the board was close to my ideal color, I repeatedly emphasized it with official color codes and visual paper samples. After months, I got a call that my board was ready to pick up. To my surprise, the board came out as almost black, not the cheerful purple that I had requested.

Inevitably, human work always has some range of errors; I get it . . .

I tried to be positive and accepted the board as it was. When I got home, I noticed that the fin box position of the board was slightly off. It would not affect the ride of the wave, but then again, once you see it, it is hard to ever unsee it.

Ahhh, details, details . . .

I started to think that people don't see those fine details or choose not to care about them for one reason or another.

I recognize the importance of viewing a project or life from both macro and micro perspectives. Being able to shift gears between the two is critical. If you only pay attention to the details and do not see the big picture, you lose sight of the overall vision. It tends to generate a perfectionist mindset of never getting anything done. However, if you only see the bigger picture and fail to pay attention to the details, you lose sensitivity and the refinements of the process.

My observation is that in our current fast-paced culture, we lose sight of details as the cost of getting things done. We are already fatigued from doing something, and no extra energy is left to care further about the details.

I remember being amazed by watching the documentary *Jiro Dreams of Sushi*, about the legendary sushi chef Jiro in Japan. He said that he spent a decade only learning how to make rice properly. As he is ninety-seven years old, when he grabs a small pinch of rice in his hand, he knows exactly how much rice makes twenty grams without pausing to think. Besides the sushi itself, his restaurant experience is thought out from beginning to end: the way the napkin is folded, the weight of the chopsticks, the temperature of the miso soup, the selection of the background music and its decibel level, the placement of the dish.

I know that paying attention to these details takes effort, patience, time, and integrity. Ignoring is much easier than spending painstaking time on minor details that few even appreciate or notice.

So why should we even bother to care?

To me, it is about principles. It is about the flavor of life.

I find joy and appreciation when someone puts extra care into something. More often than not, I don't see who made that extra effort in the results, but it makes me smile. *Someone cared.*

When I traveled to Tokyo a couple of years ago, I stayed at a local inn where they served a welcome tea upon my arrival. I witnessed how they poured warm water into a serving cup while they prepared tea. It was a slow and unhurried process done in silence. Then, the hostess emptied the warm water before pouring the tea into the cup.

I asked, "What is the purpose of pouring the warm water into the cup if you were going to empty it?" The hostess said, "To have the outside of the cup just warm enough, not too hot. That temperature will keep your hands feeling welcomed while you drink the tea."

Then, she turned the cup in the direction where I could see the most beautiful pattern on it and handed the cup to me with two hands.

I could feel a vibration of the warmth of the tea moving my entire soul. This small yet bighearted gesture inspires me to strive to do the same.

The truth is that I believe people do notice these efforts. They may not appreciate them right away, but some will.

And this is not only about a product or professional service. We could always do one percent better with how we care in our daily lives: how we interact with a stranger, how we smile a little extra, how we hold open a door for the person behind us, or how we send a thoughtful email to a friend.

An extra pinch of caring and kindness can go a long way, much more than you might think.

It takes practice. More importantly, we have to care in the first place.

Whenever I practice the piano or feel that I care less about a certain tone of the note that I play, I have to remind myself constantly: I am the one who cares about those minor details—not necessarily to show them to others, but to add more joy to my life in the first place.

When a certain phrasing of the music finally comes closer to what I envisioned, I know I have received the most by contributing to the beautiful sonic flavor of life.

How about you? When did you last notice that extra care from someone or something?

I challenge you to care one percent more about whatever you do this week. Then, pay attention to details, and appreciate when you notice another person's extra care.

Concert Corner

Notturno in G-flat Major, Op. 70, No. 1 by Giuseppe Martucci

Things That Can Only Be Seen from Afar by Nakseo Jaengi Kim

The Importance of Documenting Your Life

Last year, about this time, I purchased a five-year journal by Hobonichi. I was captivated by the idea that you could write one journal for five years. Each page has five different spaces to write for five consecutive years on the same date. The small space helps you write succinctly, yet it is big enough to ramble a bit longer if you wish. I am already excited for my future self, reading what I have written years later when I am on the same page. That means on the same page on December 16, 2028, I can see what I was thinking five years ago in 2023. Isn't that intriguing?

All my life, I have been a journal keeper. Whether that is a list of practice strategies for the day or a long, rambling entry to clear my mind, keeping a journal has been a part of my life since my youth. If there is one tool for me that shapes my life and allows me to navigate in a desired direction, I would say that is journaling.

Why journaling?

One of the benefits of journaling is documenting your life. The author of *Die with Zero*, Bill Perkins, emphasizes that your life is the sum of your experiences. This means that everything you do in life—all the daily, weekly, monthly, annual, and once-in-a-lifetime experiences you have—adds up to who you are.

People retire on their memories. When you're too frail to do much of anything else, you can still look back on the life you've lived and experience immense pride, joy, and the bittersweet feeling of nostalgia.

Experiences keep on giving in the form of fulfillment through your memories. Over time, the ongoing memory dividend can sometimes add up to more experience points than the original experience provided.

Of course, unforgettable memories live in our hearts. These can be captured in the form of videos or photos, which I take all the time as well. For me, however, the best way to capture the joy of seemingly mundane daily life and its unique offerings is by writing.

On September 13, 2023, I wrote the following: "Today, I looked at the calendar; there were zero appointments. Somehow, the space I created in my day made it possible today to be one of the most productive days, filled with things I would like to do without any deadlines. I was feeling satisfied, productive, and creative. What a power of space in your mind and life. Let's declutter the time and energy more."

I don't remember exactly what I did that day, but I distinctly remember the moment I realized that I had such an amazing day with the space of time, promising myself the power of a blank canvas. I did not write any details about the day, but I captured my moment of enlightenment for the day.

When it comes down to journaling, here are five things that I have learned that have helped my process:

1. **There is no minimum.** Years ago, I kept the "Morning Pages" practice according to the suggestion in the book *The Artist's Way*, which is to write three pages of anything each morning. As much as I loved the process and recommend that everyone try it at least once, I couldn't keep up with the three-page rule. When it comes to journaling, I like to freestyle in any way I wish. It can be a series of words, not a complete sentence. It can be just one word. We are often caught in the mindset that journaling has to be some longer writing or trying to fill the space, but when I take the pressure off from word counts and think of how I want to capture this moment and what is relevant, it becomes more fun.
2. **You need to be honest with yourself.** It is funny that no matter what method you are using, you often feel that someone will eventually read the very thing you are writing. Therefore, you keep our protective mode on, consciously or

unconsciously, holding back what you are actually thinking. However, you have to be completely honest with yourself and let your guard down. This step is especially important if you use journaling for mental clarity. Just be yourself, because journaling is for yourself. Be unfiltered.

3. **Look for a story-worthy moment in each day.** I don't write all the same things I do every single day as a daily journal entry, but I try to look for interesting thoughts or experiences in an everyday moment. Maybe I looked at the sunrise differently, had another thankful moment, taught a dog a new trick and witnessed the moment he did it (but only with a treat in my hand), or had teary eyes in a particular scene of a movie or book. When I look for those moments, it becomes easier for me to notice them.
4. **Write from a stream of consciousness.** When I feel stuck in life, I start to write what is relevant to me at that time. From there, I begin to write whatever I am thinking. This way of writing helps me to clear my mind and see myself more objectively. I recommend using a pen instead of a pencil when writing. From the beginning, you eliminate the need to erase and encourage the flow of your writing.
5. **Try using old-fashioned pen and paper.** I have a journaling app and other documenting applications that help me capture my thoughts quickly and more efficiently, but I always keep a notebook as my journaling companion.

> Taking time to sit down and write down my thoughts with a pen, even if only for a few minutes, has a therapeutic and calming effect on my mind.

For me, the best part of documenting our lives is to relive those precious moments more vividly. This has the effect of slowing down our lives.

I couldn't believe we were already in December 2023 when I looked at this month's calendar. December? Really? Then, when I read my journal entries for this year, one by one, I realized that many moments of 2023 were full of memories that I cherish. The conception of time wasn't as fast as I thought when I relived each day again. It's another life hack! That alone, for me, makes it worth journaling.

Concert Corner

"La plus que lente," L. 121 by Claude Debussy

A Snowy Path, Traced by Our Gaze by Jeonyeok ▶

20.

Simple Secrets to Reading More

Someone once advised me that if you want to read more books, you should *always carry a book with you.*

As bluntly simple as this is, for me, it has been one of the most effective tools I've found for reading more books. We have more time for reading than we perceive: waiting in a doctor's office, between meetings, waiting to board a plane at airports, or finding a corner at family holidays. While waiting for something, I can easily choose a book over a phone if I already have a book in my hand. The problem is that we usually spend more time holding a phone than a book.

I love reading. Books, fiction and nonfiction, have been among my most incredible life teachers. I get distilled wisdom from someone through nonfiction to gain a different perspective. Fiction helps deepen my emotions by allowing me to experience the characters intimately. Research suggests that devouring books helps keep the mind sharper for longer while lowering heart rate and feelings of psychological distress. *Whoa! What a wonderful bonus!*

Interestingly, I read more books in English than in Korean although Korean is much easier for me as my native language. Ironically, I published my first book, *Whenever You're Ready*, in English and then translated it into Korean to be officially published in Korea. It is funny to think that one would start this ambitious journey of writing a book in a foreign language first rather than in one's mother tongue. My only explanation is that it doesn't matter which language one writes in as long as it comes from the heart.

During the last two decades, I have trained myself to think in English, which has helped me develop a different way of thinking from my primary way of thinking in Korean. Switching between two languages has allowed me to develop my thinking muscles and perspective, improving my shortcomings in critical-thinking skills.

Last week, one of my friends asked if I had any tips on reading more books, as if I had some earth-shattering answers. The truth is that as much as I love to read, I wish I could do more of it. However, I have eight tips to share that work for me to keep more books in my life:

1. **Read a book about what you are currently interested in.** I am surprised at how often people try to read books only because they are from some bestseller lists and have nothing to do with their current interests. Though it can be fun to choose a book based on its popularity, it doesn't mean you'll enjoy reading it. Listen to your small inner voice to find out what quests interest you, and then find answers in those books. You will more likely enjoy the process because it aligns with your curiosity.

2. **Read multiple books at once.** I always have about four or five books in progress simultaneously. I am not a perfectionist when it comes to books. Start wherever you left off, catch up when you can, and ditch the book if you don't want to finish it or don't find it interesting anymore. By giving yourself permission to call it quits, you allow more space for books that you will love.

3. **Read in different formats.** I often listen to audiobooks when I drive. Despite my initial resistance, I now love reading on a Kindle for convenience. The more formats you have, including Kindle and audiobooks, the better chances you will read more.

4. **Study the table of contents.** For nonfiction, I take my time to study the table of contents and go back to this page as often as necessary to gauge the book's big picture. The author had a blueprint for thinking about its architecture

before they wrote the book. The table of contents is the main structure of the building before the decorations of the house (aka the details of the chapters) have been added. The more you see the big picture, the better you will understand the main points of the book. This is the fun factor!

5. **Start small.** Try reading fun articles or short stories in a magazine. Start by reading a set time of ten minutes every day. Read a small amount, such as one page or one chapter daily, for several weeks until you establish a good habit.

6. **Read dirty.** My books are crammed with handwritten notes, lines, and highlights on pages folded on the corners for easy access. For me, a part of the fun of reading nonfiction is discovering something that resonates with me or teaches me. The more actively engaged you are in your reading, the more likely you will retain what you read. My steps are typically 1) fold corners at pages that I find interesting on the initial reading, 2) go back to the folded page and make a line with a pen under the more important sentences, 3) highlight words or sentences with colors, and 4) write my reflection as one word or a sentence next to the highlighted section.

   This means that I go through the book multiple times with my guide to essential spots with these steps. When I return to the book years later, I look only at the pages on which I made a note or highlighted.

7. **Invest in books.** I don't have a set budget for books. I splurge on them more than on anything else in life. If I see a book that I want to read, I get it without hesitation. It adds friction to a luxurious trip to a foreign country, but sometimes, it has given me greater satisfaction and more growth. The side effects? More reading. It's a vicious, positive cycle that I don't want to get off. Afterward, I donate books to local libraries when I decide not to keep them.

8. **Track your books.** I have a Notion file in which I give scores for each book I read, a one-sentence review, and the date I started. It is not anything fancy or for sharing with others but purely for the enjoyment I get from keeping these thoughts in one place. Sometimes, just reading the title and my quick summary gives me an instant time-travel machine back to when I read the book, the smell of the place I read it in, or how I felt during the reading experience. Additionally, I keep several screenshots of the best parts of the book in the file.

I hope that some of the above points will inspire you to grab a book and start reading!

Concert Corner

"Doctor Gradus ad Parnassum" from *Children's Corner*
by Claude Debussy

Warmer than the Sun, Bigger than the Ocean
by Yoon Min Jeong (grimgrit) ▶

21.

Chopin *Is* Cool!

Last week, I had the pleasure to be a conference artist at the state conference of the Oregon Music Teachers' Association in Florence, Oregon. I started with a public presentation, followed with a masterclass, and finished with a solo piano performance of 시음 */si-úm/* (from Korean, *si* meaning "poetry" and *úm-ak* meaning "music") on the last night. I must say that it was quite intense for me because it is not that easy to switch gears from public speaker to teacher to performing artist in such a short time. Yet I felt that people really had a maximal experience of what I could offer in a diverse way. Plus, there is something very beautiful about spending days with the same group of people, having some quality and quantity of time to get into deep conversations and get to know each other well.

One of the big thoughts that I shared with fellow music

educators throughout the conference was that we all have a mission: to nurture our students to be spokespeople for and patrons of this beautiful art form of classical music. The real value of what we do is when students can translate what they learn from those music lessons and apply those artistic expressions into creating a harmonious society and make themselves healthy individuals. Those students will positively impact our community and shape our future with that musical expression.

Sometimes I am asked, "Why classical music? Why is it that you think you've been able to draw younger people into enjoying classical piano? What do you do differently?"

Many older generations experienced classical music as the main source of entertainment at home or at the local theatre when they were growing up. In our world of so much stimulation, I find that the younger generations need a little more guidance or at least the first experience of being guided into classical music. It is not that they wouldn't be interested in classical music, but they never have a chance to experience it properly. I talk to an audience like a friend who happens to be a concert pianist, as if I invited them to my living room to play a piece that I am passionate about. I assume nothing, and there are no program notes nor a list of pieces that I will play—just me on a stage with a microphone to guide and embrace it as a journey we take together. I create a bridge by sharing my feelings about the piece, as well as my struggles, victories, and stories connected to the piece.

I then open a path for them to get into their own stories and feelings about the music as they listen. My goal is to be a vessel for the music so that they can get its core message as directly as possible. The more they connect with me, the easier it is for them to bypass me, the pianist, and get to their souls, which directly communicate with the music. They finally get it when they are properly given the opportunities and they think the music of Beethoven and Chopin is cool! I believe that we don't have to change the content of classical music for a modern audience; we must simply change the wrapping paper around this amazing content as we deliver it.

About three hundred years ago, classical music was the pop music of European culture. Chopin would have been like a friend of yours introducing his new compositions at a cocktail party. But the wall between performer and audience has grown higher as time has gone on. Many unspoken rules and traditions have been created around the culture of classical music over the years. When you attend a classical concert, there are multiple assumptions: you know a lot about classical music, you should wear formal attire, you know who Chopin was, and the performer will never interact with the audience and will disappear after the concert. Program notes explain the background of the piece like a history book, and there is always an intermission of fifteen minutes after the first forty-five minutes of music, followed by another forty-five minutes of music.

As much as I am familiar with these traditions, I am also aware that these assumptions and rules could drive a potential new audience away from giving classical music a try, thinking that it is only for a certain type of people or their grandmothers. That is why I would like to break that barrier down as much as possible. I know that the content of the cup—the beauty of classical music—is timeless, but I could always change the cup to have a more contemporary look so that people would drink from it much more comfortably in this twenty-first century.

To me, classical music is a gift to humanity; it carries solace, joy, healing power, peace, and the ability to connect with others and oneself in the spirit. It is about raw human emotions that existed three hundred years ago, as we would feel the same way in the twenty-first century. I want to let people know that this amazing gift, like mountains and rivers in nature, is available to everyone. I push these boundaries so that more people can experience the beauty of classical music and benefit from it.

What about you? Do you listen to classical music? Maybe you do, or maybe you have never given this beautiful art form a proper chance. Regardless of where you stand, I would like to give you a challenge, which is to listen to one piece of classical music as a sole activity. Not as a background, not while you're in a car, but to solely listen to and focus on that music.

Closing your eyes is also a wonderful way to engage in the art. Simply take flight with the music during that listening treat. I promise it will do your soul good.

Valse in A-flat Major, Op. 42
by Frédéric Chopin

Good Morning Radio by MOSLA

“I told the universe (and anyone who would listen) that I was committed to living a creative life not in order to save the world, not as an act of protest, not to become famous, not to gain entrance to the canon, not to challenge the system, not to show the bastards, not to prove to my family that I was worthy, not as a form of deep therapeutic emotional catharsis . . . but simply because I liked it.”

—ELIZABETH GILBERT

THE THIRD MOVEMENT:

Largo appassionato

22.

Homecoming: Familiar yet Unfamiliar

I am writing this from Indianapolis, Indiana, my second home in America. I am attending a Midwest performing arts conference to share what I do as a pianist. There is a pleasant breeze in the mild, sunny weather at the end of summer. I must have caught the right time to be here—not too humid, not too hot.

The Uber driver asked me what I was filming, noticing I was taking a video from the window on our ride to the hotel. There wasn't an apparent picture-worthy scene other than green pastures, brick buildings, and two-story houses surrounded by big trees. There's just something about the green colors in summer here, which are much lusher than in San Diego. I smiled and said, "Indiana."

Having returned to Indiana a handful of times since moving to Southern California almost nine years ago, I notice conflicting emotions arising whenever I visit this home state. This might be similar to seeing my small hometown in South Korea during my early childhood.

Familiar yet unfamiliar, new and shiny modern buildings have replaced the ones I used to know. Many of the people I hung out with are no longer here, though a few still are. Most strangely, despite all my memories in this space, I find that I have dramatically changed into someone I wouldn't have recognized back when I lived here.

This realization isn't good or bad; it just is. It feels weird that I can drive to places without GPS in Indianapolis or Bloomington, yet I no longer recognize them anymore by their landmarks.

A hundred years from now, perhaps three to five hundred years from now, this place may look completely different. People I used to know will be long gone, including myself. The things that I care about will have been forgotten and become dust in the universe. The foods I used to love, the memories I cherished, the people I loved, and the music I used to make—none of these will matter to anyone.

After a long day at the conference, a woman asked me what my plan was for the rest of the day. I said I would go to Butler University and practice for a couple of hours. She was surprised by my answer. "You mean now?" she asked. "Aren't you tired?"

The truth is I *was* a bit tired, yet I wanted to practice some—not because I wanted to prove anything to anyone or because I had an immediate deadline that I needed to meet for my concert schedule, but because this was another first day of the rest of my life. I desired to feel the music, especially after such a long day.

When I think of how things are constantly changing and how I will be forgotten in hundreds of years, I get the urge to enjoy the details of the moments that life offers. How I live my life today, how I interact with people, how I enjoy the things I love, how I express my love for people, and how I appreciate the food that I eat are what matter now, in this moment, the most.

Macro and micro: Focus on this moment, each step, but don't forget the big picture as you go on, existing in the passage of time. I try to make this delicate balancing act my compass for navigating this life.

Whenever I feel behind on my practice schedule for upcoming performances or overwhelmed by the workload, I remind myself that nature doesn't hurry, yet everything is accomplished. The flowers that we see seem to happen overnight, but they have been making their way all along for months.

It's just like the saying: "Before enlightenment, chop wood, carry water. After enlightenment, chop wood, carry water." Perhaps my version might be, "Before enlightenment, play piano. After enlightenment, play piano."

This poem, an excerpt from "The Eighth Elegy" of Rainer Maria Rilke's *Duino Elegies*, resonated with me this week:

If no one else, the dying must notice
how unreal, how full of pretense,
is all that we accomplish here,
where nothing is allowed to be itself.

Oh hours of childhood, when behind each shape
more than the past appeared
and what streamed out before us
was not the future.

We take the very young child
and force it around, so that it sees objects —
not the Open, which is so deep
in animals' faces. Free from death.

We, only, can see death;
the free animal has its decline in back of it, forever,
and God in front, and when it moves,
it moves already in eternity, like a fountain.

. . . it feels its life as boundless,
unfathomable, and without regard
to its own condition: pure, like its outward gaze.

And where we see the future,
it sees all time
and itself within all time,
forever healed.

The part "it moves already in eternity, like a fountain . . . its life as boundless" strikes me like lightning. I had to read the poem aloud multiple times to absorb the presence of the words and take it all in. This has been a transformative poem for me in many respects.

I am now curious. What would your action be like to the quote that I shared?

"Before enlightenment, ______________________________.

After enlightenment, ______________________________."

I hope you get to do that today.

Concert Corner

Arabeske in C Major, Op. 18 by Robert Schumann

Hope III by Jed Dorsey

23.

The Art of Becoming

Over the past year, I've had the privilege of being the writer of a memoir of a close friend of mine, who is ninety-one years old. When he asked me to be the writer for this passion project, I was hesitant to accept the challenge. *Will I be able to express authentically what he went through?* I wondered. *Can I be a good messenger for someone else?* Despite my doubts, in the end, I said yes. He convinced me that he was not looking for the best writer in this world to deliver his story, but for his friend, Jeeyoon, to be in that role. He trusted my willingness to do my best and my ability to connect with music and, ultimately, to his story.

Writing for someone else is different from writing your own story. Instead of thinking about who I am, I needed to imagine my thoughts and emotions as if I were someone else. I had to recreate the scenes in my head like a movie from the mosaic puzzles that he provided. Someone born in 1934 went through the Great Depression, World War II, the Vietnam War, the dramatic changes of social justice, and digital advances from letters being the only form of communication to bulky computers and then to smartphones—computers in our pockets. I can't imagine what it must have been like growing up in a small town in Michigan where houses had no running water and becoming someone full of rich life experiences and still living a great, healthy life at ninety-one in California.

He said, "I often shake my head at what has happened to me to allow me to live the life I am living now."

I had a wonderful time reliving his cherished memories through this project. How many people can live to their nineties, still look back, articulate their emotions, and share wisdom from their life experiences? I was privileged to participate in this project and learned much from the process. The book's title is *Ever the Beginning*, which fits his life motto. Each day he encounters is the new beginning of an adventure and his transformation. He says curiosity was one of the most important compasses in his life, which caused him to become who he is now.

While writing his story, I couldn't help but imagine what I will be like when I am ninety-one. What stories would I tell to someone? Beyond the wrinkles and apparent physical decline, who would I become inside? Would my close friends still be around? What memories would I keep reliving in my mind to savor once again?

I always thought I was lucky to have significant landmarks in my life—beyond personal events like graduation or the fortieth birthday—through the release of my albums. Interestingly, in each album release (which happens every two or three years), I have encountered myself as someone more mature, someone slightly different from the previous version of myself.

Famous pianists often release the same collections of Beethoven sonatas or specific repertoires recorded once again in old age. For example, the renowned pianist Alfred Brendel recorded the complete Beethoven sonatas during his career in his thirties, forties, and again in his sixties. When you directly compare the repertoire of his recording in his early thirties with that in his early seventies, you might wonder if that is even the same musician. The difference is not necessarily good or bad; it is simply different. Perhaps *transformation* is a better word to describe this process. Although I appreciate the youthful energy contained in the early recordings, I often enjoy the more layered, complex emotions I hear in the later ones.

Even though you might not have your own musical albums to reflect on, we all know that feeling of transformation in how we become someone different from our twenties and our forties to our seventies and beyond. What intrigues me is that we don't feel this progress of change daily, even though we are constantly becoming someone slightly different, even though these changes usually happen in micro steps.

However, there is always that day you feel significant growth: The day you don't cry anymore from telling your heartbreaking story to someone. The day you can run more miles without stopping and taking a break. The day you don't care what others think about you anymore. The day you can finally forgive someone from the bottom of your heart.

When you look back at those moments, each transformation feels like a milestone.

We are on the journey of becoming. Life has a constant forward momentum. I wish to keep my heart open and my mind flexible enough to adapt and grow as I age. I want to be able to change my view, listen to opposite opinions, and constantly learn a new, better way to live life.

Life is, after all, the art of becoming.

As my ninety-one-year-old friend advised, curiosity might be key in this process.

I am curious about who I will become.

I am curious what tomorrow might hold for me.

I am curious how you will transform yourself.

Concert Corner

"Clair de lune" from *Suite Bergamasque* by Claude Debussy

Twilight Together at Masian Beach by Nana

NANA

24.

Design Your Day

Last week, I celebrated my forty-third birthday (ah, already? Time flies). Even though the number of my age has not affected me in any way, the way I approach my birthday has changed over the last decade. I remember several birthdays in my twenties and early thirties that ended rather gloomily. It could be because my boyfriend or close friends forgot it was my birthday, or I dismissed the day as a typical mundane workday.

Then, one year in my mid-thirties, I decided to do my birthday differently. I would design that day exactly how I wanted it to be, decide on how I want to spend the time, whom I want to spend it with, and what I wanted to eat or do.

No one needed to do anything extra to make me feel special. I depended only on myself for the enjoyment that day. I willingly took on that role and helped myself to spend it in the way I knew I would enjoy.

That very experience has taught me many lessons: *I am in charge of my happiness, no one else. If I know how to design my day in the best possible way for me, then I know how to treat myself well for the other 364 days. My preference is not selfish but is a duty to myself. It doesn't take much to make myself happy; it is often an experience, not a thing.*

Last week, I called my surfing coach, whom I hadn't seen for over eight months.

"Michelle! Are you available next Wednesday? I would love to surf with you."

I didn't tell her that it was my birthday, but I knew I would love to start the day surfing with her. Luckily, she was available! For the first time, I took out my custom board from the legendary shaper Skip Frye. I had had it for more than four months but had never ridden it. I decided to finally take it to the local surf break, Terramar, in Carlsbad, California. I hadn't intentionally waited until my birthday to ride it, but I did wait purposely until I felt ready to honor the world-class board.

That beautiful summer morning in southern California with gentle two- to three-foot waves was perfect. The board cut through the water like butter, gliding smoothly. The waves I caught that day were like a special gift that nature endowed me with and were absolutely joyous. I laughed and smiled like a kid on a playground.

The rest of the day was filled with a delicious sushi lunch with close friends, playing with doggies, a relaxed walk around the quiet neighborhood, and playing one of my favorite board games, Dixit.

In the evening, my boyfriend asked whether I wanted to watch a movie, and I said, "Nah . . . Let's just talk. Tell me some stories!" I pulled up a blanket to my chin and gave him a big smile. We chatted for a while until my eyes got heavy with sleep. We talked about things I had already forgotten, silly things, funny stories, music, surfing, travel, food, and life.

My birthday was filled with love, joy, gratitude, laughter, friends, music, and nature. It was a beautifully designed day for me to appreciate life. What a joy it was! I promised myself that I shall repeat it on days that are not birthdays.

When was the last time you planned your day intentionally by listening to yourself? What did it include?

My wish for your special day: You get to design your birthday exactly how you would like and then enjoy it fully.

Concert Corner

"Des Abends" ("In the Evening") from *Fantasiestücke*, Op. 12
by Robert Schumann

A Wish Lifted to the Stars by Jeonyeok ▶

25.

Yes, Absolutely—or No

There is always something we are asked to do more than we would like. We are often guilty of saying yes to something we feel half-hearted about and end up doing a half-hearted attempt. I have learned this lesson from my experiences, especially with a project that initially sounded good. It resulted in taking my energy and time away from the project I really wanted to devote time and energy to.

It is no one else's job but mine to know what excites me about work. Derek Sivers, the author of *Hell Yeah or No*, recommends that if you're not feeling "Hell yeah, that would be awesome!" about something, say no. The answer is always intuitive and quick, spoken by your inner voice. If you don't feel genuine enthusiasm, say no to almost everything. This will free your time and mind.

However, there is value in saying yes when someone is starting their career. It adds variety and helps you figure out your preferences. I became more certain about who I am after many years of taking work that didn't excite me but taught me valuable lessons. One of the beauties of getting old is that we can navigate our lives more efficiently from the wisdom we gain from youth.

When I say yes to something I am genuinely excited about, I will make space in life to give it my full attention. As Sivers says, "Saying no makes your yes more powerful." This kind of decision-making has helped me to shape life with focus and joy. If my day is filled with more absolutely *yes* decisions, I own the decisions and have fun. If I said yes to an hour of piano practice, I would give myself entirely to it. There is no place in this world I need to be other than on the piano bench.

I try to avoid ambivalence, or saying yes but doing a half-hearted job even if I fully committed myself to yes. Generally speaking, I love complexity and duality, which is perfectly fine for staying in the gray zone. Yet I've learned that fully owning my choices has shown me a pathway to happiness; I say no to many things, but for those things I say yes to, I do them all the way.

Does your *yes* list reflect who you are and how you direct your life? I hope that your day is filled with your *yes* choices and that you have fun on the playground of life.

Sonata in E Major, K. 380 (L. 23) by Domenico Scarlatti

To You Who Brighten My Day by Gobom

26.

Notes to My Younger Self

Last week, while walking along a snowy sidewalk in New York City, my head was filled with a request I'd gotten from the Music Teachers National Association's *Business Digest* online journal. They had asked me to respond in under five minutes to the following three prompts:

1. Describe your current career.
2. What are the key steps or experiences that helped guide you to where you are now?
3. What advice do you have for others who may hope to follow a similar path?

My initial thought was, *No problem! I could talk about this topic for hours!* Then, I realized it was much harder to narrow it down to only five minutes rather than hours. In fact, giving an answer to the seemingly simple question "How do you do what you do?" would not be that easy for me. I realized that my career is like a complicated web spinning from the core mission of being a classical pianist, which includes teaching, podcasting, performing, writing, speaking, coaching, creating online content, marketing, presenting concerts, and recording albums.

At the same time, this is exactly why this journal wanted to feature me in their article as a new model for an entrepreneur musician in the twenty-first century. Unlike two hundred years ago, being an excellent musician alone might not be enough to thrive in the current era.

I feel *imposter syndrome* whenever I have the opportunity to give advice to other musicians who want to do what I do. What worked for me might not work for their paths. However, when I think about what I would advise the twenty-year-old younger version of myself, knowing what I know now, it feels easier to give some tips to the younger me.

So here are the top ten pieces of advice I would give to others who may hope to follow a similar path of being a musician in the twenty-first century:

1. Don't wait for opportunities to come to you; create your own. No one will knock on your practice room door and

beg to fulfill your dreams. The more proactive you are, the better the chances that you will become lucky. After all, you create your own luck.

2. Follow your curiosity and just *do it*. Curiosity is the inner compass of your interest and passion. Try to listen to that small voice within; then, take a tiny step into whatever that might be today. In the process, you will learn what works for you and what doesn't. Remember that you can only steer a ship if it's moving.
3. Know your why. Just like a company, your brand (yourself) needs a mission statement about what you believe in and how you hope to serve others. Imagine you have everything you hope for regarding money, time, and energy right now. What would you do to express yourself and serve others?
4. Redefine your idea of success. First, get in tune with yourself. Then, figure out what makes you happy, and do that every day. Find your contentment without needing the approval of society or others.
5. Build your own community. If I had to distill everything I do down to one word, it would be *connection*. Create your community using various methods, such as newsletters, online content, in-person concerts, family and friends, colleagues, professional contacts, fans, and whoever believes in what you do. Then, nurture that connection with genuine care and love regularly and continuously.

6. When you are afraid of doing something, know that it is exactly what you should face. Sometimes fear indicates life telling you that this is a time for learning and growing. I remember having to take uncomfortable and fearful steps that I didn't want to take. Trust me. Your future self will thank you.

7. You are a unique messenger. No matter what you do, no one in this world is like you. You don't have to create the most exotic thing in this world to be creative. You are enough, just as you are. Simply be a unique messenger through how you see the world.

8. Don't stop practicing, no matter what concert, album, or projects are presented for you at this moment or not. In the meantime, keep practicing for yourself, even when you don't have any concert engagements. When the opportunity comes at the right time in your life, you will be happy that you are ready to share with others. I know this is easier said than done because it takes daily discipline, but this is an important step for you to continue as a performing artist. Keep the momentum going.

9. Pay as much attention to your mind and body as you do to your work. Exercise regularly, meditate, eat healthy foods, and constantly hunt for your method of finding peace. On this path, at the end of the day, you will have to pick yourself

up over and over again. A healthy mind and body will help you stay positive during stormy periods.

10. Stay humble, yet encourage yourself with positive affirmations. This is a delicate dance on and off the stage of performance. You can't be too proud, but you need to take time to celebrate. You can't be too egoistic, yet you must trust yourself to do the work well. If you understand that you are merely one puzzle piece in the big picture of the universe, you might be able to find this balance better.

I hope this list gives you a guiding light to inspire whatever you do on your career path.

Concert Corner

"Pagodes" from *Estampes* by Claude Debussy

When the Sky Holds the Sea by Mclalan ▶

27.

Start Small; Win Big

This week, I was reminded of the concept of keystone habits and their importance. Journalist Charles Duhigg introduced this idea in his book *The Power of Habit*. The term *keystone* refers to the central stone that holds an arch together. *Keystone habits*, then, are minor changes or routines that can trigger a positive ripple effect in other areas of a person's life, much like the first domino piece. I especially love the idea that introducing one small habit can result in several big things taking care of themselves.

For me, regular exercise is undoubtedly one of the most significant keystone habits that has a clear domino effect. This could range from hard weight-training for an hour to a relaxing stretch on a mat for ten minutes or a stroll around the neighborhood.

Moving my body has always had the most positive effect on my mind. Because I exercise regularly, my natural inclination is to eat healthy foods. Since I feel better, I have better energy throughout the day. When in doubt, I move my body, and, sure enough, I always feel at least one percent better afterward, whatever that movement might have been.

Another simple keystone action I find helpful is making my bed. Could making your bed result in more happiness? According to Gretchen Rubin, author of *The Happiness Project*, the answer is yes, it can! While researching her book, Rubin found that one of the most common simple changes that led to happiness was learning to make one's bed each morning. Interestingly, she said that, in addition to overall happiness, bedmakers are more likely to enjoy their jobs, feel motivated to exercise regularly, and feel well rested.

I am not sure whether all those significant results can be attributed to making your bed, but I surely notice that it does add an overall positive feel to the room that I frequently pass by throughout the day.

Here are seven more ideas for top keystone habits that you might want to try:

1. **Plan your day:** Taking a few minutes to prioritize my to-do list and planning the day in the morning or, better yet, in the evening before going to bed adds a noticeable value to my day.
2. **Establish daily routines:** It might not sound sexy or

spontaneous to stick to the same rituals every day, but that is precisely what many successful people do. Just sticking to morning rituals and night routines before going to bed makes me feel more creative throughout the day. It sounds ironic, but I feel that I can fly higher by setting boundaries.

3. **Go to bed early:** This sometimes requires conscious effort from me. But whenever I go to bed earlier than 10 p.m., I feel rested and have a longer deep sleep time, more energy, and better focus the next day.
4. **Cook a healthy meal for myself:** Honestly, I can't say that I am good at cooking, especially when it comes to preparing an elaborate meal for others. However, I regularly cook meals for myself all the time. Brussels sprouts, carrots, and salmon drizzled with olive oil and sea salt and cooked in an air fryer are my ready-to-go healthy meal. I feel the best when I eat nutritious meals at home.
5. **Meditate and focus on breathwork:** I like to "habit stack" my breathwork with my morning routine of stretching, planning my day, and journaling. Who says you have to make each keystone habit separate? Deep breathing, with ten slow inhales and exhales, contributes to a relaxed mind for me.
6. **Stretch:** These days, I place a yoga mat open by the bed before going to sleep and slowly roll over to the mat like a sloth when I wake up. Three to five minutes of whatever feel-good movement on the mat first thing in the morning

makes a world of difference for me. The key here is to reduce the hesitation in having to open a yoga mat as soon as I wake up in the morning. It is already there before my mind starts to make up excuses.

7. **Practice piano in the morning:** This might not apply to you, but whenever I practice piano in the morning, I feel positive and am at my productive best throughout the day. Whichever activity requires the most brainpower for you, try to do it in the morning.

Fantaisie-Impromptu in C-sharp Minor, Op. 66 by Frédéric Chopin

Even the Sunset Smiles upon Us by Jeonyeok ▶

28.

Is It Okay to Be Mediocre?

When I started surfing several years ago, I felt full of promise and excitement about something new, something completely different from playing the piano. Turns out I had no idea what I was about to face.

Just like any other project, I faced surfing with a strong work ethic, discipline, and a systematic approach. I hired the champion pro surfer Michelle Bautista Layton as my coach, watched hundreds of videos, and read books about surfing. I analyzed what could be better and how I was doing every time I went out to surf, and I mind-surfed when I was out of town for concerts.

I am not sure what I expected, but I thought I could become good at surfing, like those videos of surfers gliding down the perfectly shaped waves and graciously walking on the board. Those surfers make surfing look easy and seamless.

Unlike my fantasy, every time I saw photos or videos of me surfing, I was in shock. I had an awkward pose—like a *kook*, which is a derogatory term for a complete beginner surfer with those poo stances. That was *not* how I thought I looked or surfed in my head. I was constantly hard on myself for not being the best.

I should be able to do x, y, and z by now. What is wrong with me?

The ocean beat me up hard. For the past two years, I've had a foot injury, a broken nose (yup . . . I know . . .), collisions with other surfers, and two ER visits due to hits by my board. Surprisingly, those injuries happened on one- or two-foot gentle-wave days, not head-high dangerous waves I have no business being on anyway.

As many people expected, every time I was beaten by surfing with an injury, I contemplated quitting surfing. *Maybe it is too dangerous and unfit for a concert pianist whose body is an asset for what she does . . .*

Still, every time after thinking hard, I picked up the board and went out with a smile to surf again. *Let me try it one more time.*

Mostly, I didn't want my fear to be the deciding factor. Surfing isn't the only dangerous thing in my life. I could die by walking on a sidewalk! I still have to live life. With the challenge of uncertainty in life, I became at peace with the fact that I needed to be *wise*: Don't go out when the waves are too big for you, don't go to the advanced break that you are not ready for, don't go out when you're tired, wear protective gear from head to toe, keep learning to be better, and play it safely.

However, do you know what was the biggest challenge of surfing for me in the end?

It wasn't the fear of an injury. It wasn't the challenge of the sport of surfing.

It was embracing being mediocre at something.

What is so hard about that, you ask? I don't know, but it was the hardest thing to accept. Accepting that I could be bad at something bothered me greatly. I saw myself as a superwoman who could do everything well. And I was falling short big-time in surfing.

Interestingly, once I embraced my mediocre self (even if that meant I would be a novice surfer for the rest of my life), a huge sense of relief washed over me.

I told myself, *Let it be okay. Have fun. Feel the water. Be in nature. Just play like a kid in a playground.* No one should judge how we play in our lives, and I certainly shouldn't do that to myself.

Who told you that you need to be an *A* student at everything? How suffocating is that? What is wrong with being mediocre, even if you have done something for years or even for your entire life?

Someone in the audience at my last concert said to me, "You must be a really good surfer by now."

I smiled and proudly told him, "Ha, you should see me in the water. I am pretty bad. In fact, I might be a danger to the lineup sometimes. But I enjoy it."

Last week, I caught three waves in a two-hour surfing session.

It was a beautiful morning session. I screamed like a kid with every wave I caught. More than one wave per session is a huge success for me. Waiting for waves to come, I watched pelicans dive vertically from the sky and run up with a fish in their mouth. At one moment, a tiny little fish jumped out of the ocean and landed on my board before squirming back into the water. The horizon dramatically changed its ray of color from orange to yellow over the sunrise.

Through surfing, I realize that I am learning one of the most important lessons in life: Be humble, and enjoy life more like a five-year-old, without the thinking and judgmental side awakening. I understand that for some people, it takes more practice to bring out that five-year-old playful mindset once they become adults. But don't you agree that life has more laughter with that playfulness?

What is the thing for you that you are proudly mediocre at but enjoy nonetheless?

"Jardins sous la pluie" ("Gardens in the Rain") from *Estampes* by Claude Debussy

Ocean Elegance by Art Rider

@ART
RIDER

29.

Don't Wait

A few weeks ago, I heard the news that North Korea had destroyed one of the main roads connected to South Korea. It was a road built before the Korean War (also known as the Korean Civil War, 1950–1953), when only one Korea existed.

My grade school often had mandatory drills to prepare us for a potential war. We would go under our desks, cover our heads during a particular siren, and stay there until our teacher told us to come out. I remember thinking it was fun, giggling with the other kids underneath the desks. Without going through a war in my lifetime, all the warnings and drills were like the fable of The Boy Who Cried Wolf. *Nothing will happen.* Everything in our daily lives was too peaceful to imagine a war. *Our soldiers will protect us from dangerous North Koreans if there is any attack!*

On a sunny, lazy afternoon, I was hanging around my house with my grandma. Lying next to her, I watched her knitting a scarf, mesmerized by her movement. Then, all of a sudden, my seven-year-old mind was struck by curiosity about her past. *Wait, where is her mom? Does she have a sibling?*

Sitting up straight on the floor next to my granny, I asked her, "Grandma, where is your mom? Do you have sisters or brothers?"

She paused her hands and made a mysterious facial expression as she looked outside the window. I couldn't tell if she was sad or mad. After a while, she started to move her hands again, looking down. She said, "Yes, I have my mommy. I hope she is well. Oh, I wish I could see her once again. I have two sisters and one brother. I am the youngest of my family."

She then continued to tell her story. She was born in a small town several hours from Pyongyang, the capital of North Korea. Her father was a farmer. They weren't rich but had enough to eat three meals a day. She went to a village school with her siblings. Simply sharing steamed corn on an outside table with everyone in the family was like a fun party.

There was nothing unusual about her upbringing. It was filled with the average events of daily life growing up as a kid in a small village. Then, one autumn day, there was an uneasy air in the neighborhood. Everyone seemed to be hurried and unsettled. The rumor spread quickly in the village, saying that a civil war might be taking place soon—as in immediately. Everyone seemed panicked, looking to gather their families and make an emergency plan. They spoke eagerly, exchanging rumors and ideas, saying they had better move toward the south within several hours.

Within an hour, a group of people started walking toward the south. My grandma, who was fifteen years old, joined the initial big group of neighbors. Her parents hurried her out of the house, saying that the rest of her family would join her as soon as her sisters returned from the school. They also needed a bit more time to pack for the family. Her mom said that they could easily meet her in the next town that night or the next day.

My grandma wasn't happy about the separation, but at the same time, there was no chance to make an excuse in that situation. Her neighbor from the initial group was like her aunt. She told Grandma everything would be okay. Grandma kept looking back at the crowd behind her. Her house was getting smaller and smaller with each step she took. She thought, *Mom, promise me you will find me soon!*

The group walked all night and arrived in another city. That is when she heard bombs and the sound of shooting at night. Indeed, it sounded like the beginning of something terrible. And it was. That was the first day of the Korean Civil War.

From that day on, no one could walk across the border between North and South Korea. Officially, it was divided into two countries. Unfortunately, Grandma's mom, dad, sisters, and brother were unable to make the trip down south in time. From then on, she was an orphan although she had a living family—somewhere. (Hopefully still . . .)

I lost my words about what to say to Granny at that moment. I looked at the trees outside, as she did. This wasn't what I expected to hear when I asked about her family. *How do you continue to live after something like that? How can you ever find happiness again?*

The next time I had a war drill at school, I didn't giggle underneath the desk anymore. Instead, I prayed that Granny's family was well and safe and that one day, Granny could get to see her mom again, too.

Grandma said she fought with her brother the night before she left. It was over a dried persimmon that she had eaten without his permission. She said, "I would give him all the persimmons in the world if I could see him again. I would tell him I didn't mean to eat the persimmon he had saved for later. I would say sorry. I would hug him and tell him how much I love him."

I felt an ache in my chest, listening to her talk. At that moment, she looked fifteen years old—just a young girl who missed her family. The word *sadness* cannot even come close to what I saw in her face.

I hugged Granny. I promised her that I would not wait to tell anyone to whom I needed to say, "I love you." I promised her I wouldn't fight with my brother and would tell her family what she said if I saw them later.

Several years ago, I received a phone call from Korea that my grandma had passed away at the age of ninety-seven. She waited her whole lifetime, but the day never came—the day she could meet her family once again and say, "I love you."

Now, promise me.

Don't wait.

Concert Corner

Vocalise, Op. 34, No. 14 by Sergei Rachmaninoff

Lost in Conversation, Time Flew By by oc.ssc ▶

30.

How Do I Find My Passion?

Sometimes, people comment that I am lucky to have found my passion in life. Some have asked for advice about how to help their children find their life paths. It is true that I found one of my passions—music—early on, but the story certainly doesn't end there. There are so many misconceptions about passion! People think (or want to believe) that one is born with it. There is a lightbulb moment at some point in your life, and you know what that passion is for you. Yes, your aptitude is an important factor in navigating life. However, I've found that passion is not as simple as many people may think.

According to Seth Godin, the author of *The Practice*, the strategy of "seeking one's calling" gives people a marvelous place to hide, adding that many people use it as an excuse not to act on some difficult tasks. Our passion is simply the work we've trusted ourselves to do. It requires us to do the work first. We can only steer the ship if it is moving. But I also understand that taking action without certainty is difficult. After all, who wants to do difficult work that doesn't fulfill us? Who wants to commit to a journey before they know that it's what they're meant to do?

Godin says that the trap is that only after we do the difficult work does it become our calling. Only after we trust the process does it become our passion. He says that "do what you love" is for amateurs; "love what you do" is the mantra for professionals.

You have to put in the work, invest time and energy, research, and learn the process. There is no one method to discover your passion, and there is no one passion per person. You will have plenty. But there is beauty about acting as if you're on to something, as if it will work, and as if you have a right to be here.

As Godin says, you can discover what doesn't work on your way to finding out what does. With every concert that I prepare for and every project that I create, I am not sure they'll work. People might not like or be interested in them. Often, when I receive the most positive comments about one of my newsletters, that is also when I get the highest number of people who unsubscribe from it!

I cannot please everyone. However, the key I learned is that *I* care. It is more important that I care about what I create, love the process of creating music, and believe that I make a difference even with the slightest contribution to the world.

So here it is—the essential formula that I've found works to help me discover my passion:

Love the process.
Don't care about the outcome.
Refine the process.
Repeat the process.
Care about the details (even when others don't).
Be of service.
Make things better.
Just begin the work.

Susan Kare, the designer of the original Mac interface, said that "you can't really decide to paint a masterpiece. You just have to think hard, work hard, and try to make a painting that you care about. Then, if you're lucky, your work will find an audience for whom it's meaningful."

I wish there were more guaranteed routes to finding your passion. But at the very least, we know that this works. But first, you have to be courageous enough to believe in yourself that you are enough.

Commitment to the process is the only alternative to the lottery mindset of hoping for the luck of getting picked by the universe.

Concert Corner

Nocturne in D-flat Major, Op. 27, No. 2 by Frédéric Chopin

In Gentle Light by Kaoru Yamada

"You have everything you need to
make magic. You always have.
Go make a ruckus.
The magic is that there is no magic.
Start where you are.
Don't stop."

—**SETH GODIN** FROM *THE PRACTICE*

THE FOURTH MOVEMENT:

Andante

31.

Feed Yourself a Compliment Vitamin

There is often a guest book at my concerts that people can leave messages in. I started this tradition about six years ago, realizing that I could never have enough time to connect with people after a concert. I wish I could have hours to interact and listen to their experiences as an audience. The reality is that I have only about one or two minutes to connect with each person waiting in line to greet me in the lobby after the concert. Sometimes, those lines can get long; it may take another hour or so for me to meet each audience member waiting in line!

This is where the guest book comes in handy after the crowds disappear. Letting people write notes allows me to take time later to savor their notes individually. Allow me to share a few of my favorite messages:

- "Not only are you a superb pianist; you are the most sensitive person with the rare gift of unifying the correspondence of art, poetry, and classical music into an inspiring message of love and hope." —Pamela and Jean-Pierre Amor
- "I think everyone in the audience was touched by your vulnerability and openness. You made all of us in the audience feel that we were participants rather than just spectators." —Shaun Tomson
- "I never experienced anything like your concert last night. It was like the music flowed through me and I could be detached from the world yet completely attached to the music." —Ben Christner
- "Mesmerizing! I can't actually think of words to describe how unique and exceptional you really are. Thank you." —Julie Anderson

Over the years, these guest books with positive notes have become a lifesaver whenever I feel discouraged and need a pick-me-up. On those gloomy days when I wake up lacking the enthusiasm to dive into the day, I read these notes to remind myself that what I do makes a difference to the world.

I've heard that a person needs to create at least five or six positive statements to counteract one negative statement. That means unless we consciously give energy to the positive mindset, we naturally tend to be negative. How often do we face doubt, uncertainty, criticism, and judgment, not only from outside but also from ourselves? Since we are prone to remembering and generating negative voices, we must create a system of collecting positive words on those rainy days. I am not saying that we need validation from others to boost our self-worth. Yet we can use every ounce of positive fuel, clinging to the light for use on our darkest days.

We receive positive and meaningful comments throughout our lives. The problem is that those messages, like other things in life, become forgotten after a momentary energy boost. The author of *Someday Is Today*, Matthew Dicks, recommends that we try to preserve the contents of compliments (verbally or via email, text message, or comment on social media) and schedule their return. Here's how. First, create a folder or document to save your compliments in one place. Second, if you do it via email, use the snooze function in the email application to schedule a message to arrive in the future.

Like Dicks, I collect positive notes in one file, but I've never tried to schedule an email for its return in the future. What a brilliant idea! I am already excited to see it come back to me. As Dicks says, "Positivity on the way, someday, hopefully just when I need it."

I have another suggestion: that you become someone who gives compliments to other people in the first place. When you feel something genuinely positive, don't be stingy by holding it back.

Splurge, express, and give that energy back to the universe. In our interaction of flowing positive energy, we lift up each other and ourselves in the process.

Even Nürnberg After a Meal
by Yeono

ZUM ALBRECHT
DURER HAUS.
NÜRNBERG
2024 06.5
STAEDTLER CALLIGRAPHY
PIGMENT PEN.

32.

How to Be in the Now

My performance season has taken off with the strongest force in the past few months. Last month alone, I have been to Calgary (Canada), Red Bluff and Tehama (California), Austin (Texas), and South Korea for my debut concert at the JCC Arts Center. Yet the most rigorous tour schedule just started a couple of days ago, which is the seventeen-city Midwest concert tour in thirty days. I will be driving five to seven hours on average between the venues. As I write this, I am waiting to catch a flight from the Chicago airport to Green Bay, Wisconsin, for tomorrow's concert in Marinette.

This tour has been wild, raw, new, adventurous, demanding, challenging, rewarding, grateful, interesting, exciting, freezing cold, fun, homesick, and everything beyond that I can't describe in words.

This is by far the most concerts I've given in such a short time. *Seventeen concerts in one month? Can I handle this?*

When this opportunity was presented to me, at first, I was hesitant as I anticipated the physical and mental demands of the tour. But I went for it because I was curious to discover the person I'd become after these performances—especially how strong this experience would make me as both a performer and a person.

I am at the beginning of this tour, so I am not yet in the position to report how it has affected me. In the meantime, while trying to catch a breath between these travels, my main question has been, *How can I be at peace in the present moment and still absorb all that happens in the once-in-a-life opportunity of this unique experience?*

As much as it may sound adventurous, it has been challenging for me to focus on being completely present in the now and enjoying every moment. I have always been on the go, getting ready for the next thing on the agenda. I find that my best self is elusive. One moment, I may have it; another moment, I may lose it. I have been experimenting with several things that seem to be helpful in my quest to focus on and enjoy the present moment.

First off, I have been trying to do things in silence. I typically like to listen to podcasts, music, or YouTube videos while I get ready or do nonessential activities. I realized that I am used to having background noise while I do things. When I turn off the noise that makes my brain work unconsciously, I feel more space in my brain, and activities seem to take on a slower pace. Is it a bit boring? Yes, but it helps me to be more conscious of what I am doing in the current moment. That is the price I am willing to pay for now.

Second, I start my day with ten minutes of stretching or yoga before I check my phone. I've noticed that when I start my day with checking the phone first, my brain seems to work inefficiently because my body and mind are not quite ready to be in work mode. Even if I'm just checking the phone for cute cat videos, my eyes and body suffer a bit, which affects the overall mood of the rest of the day. The best method for me is to keep the phone in airplane mode and put it far from the bed while I sleep.

These simple yet powerful adjustments have been doing wonders for me this week. I am hoping they will have a compound effect on my efforts to be in the now—peacefully and fully.

Concert Corner

Prelude No. 1 (Allegro ben ritmato e deciso) by George Gershwin

Cradled by the Ocean by Hye Park ▶

33.

I Am Transformed

I have been pacing around my house, doing not particularly important things: mopping the floor, reorganizing the closets, doing the laundry, watering the plants, and organizing my old files. I don't remember the last time I had this amount of time—maybe a year ago, maybe two years ago. There is certainly an illusion that time seems to be going more slowly when you finally stop running from place to place, driving hundreds and thousands of miles in between.

I finally came home from the seventeen-concert Midwest tour a few days ago. The last five concerts (mostly in Montana) took place in a real winter wonderland covered in snow, with temperatures averaging minus two to plus five degrees Fahrenheit (minus nineteen to minus fifteen degrees Celsius)! The unusual brisk air in San Diego (in the low fifties Fahrenheit, about twelve degrees Celsius), which many people describe as cold, feels like a hot summer breeze to me right now.

What was the tour of performing seventeen concerts in a month like? What did I learn? How am I now? What kind of experiences did I have? What was my favorite? These questions constantly, involuntarily resound in my head, yet I can't find answers, as if my thoughts and experiences are still in the air, taking time to settle down to earth.

There are several things that I am noticing, though. The first is that I have renewed energy. I thought that once I was back home, I would not do anything but sleep for hours and hours, but no. Instead, I am pacing around the house, organizing, working out, exploring a new repertoire, playing my current program slowly and thoroughly, and thinking about new projects. Maybe something about being in new places and new experiences gives you a mental break in life. Maybe this is a heightened level of gratitude for your environment, too: your piano, your favorite home meals, your morning routine, and your bed (oh, how much I missed it!).

Second, I still don't have a sense of days. I'm sure that will change soon. But for a month, there weren't any weekends or Mondays or Wednesdays to me, simply a day when I had a performance or a day when I didn't have a performance. It is interesting to live life without those lines between days.

Nor did I keep count of the concerts. Instead, I let myself exist in the space of creating music indefinitely. This made for a simpler existence. A day always began with a new focus, new audience, new piano, and new adjustment to a different environment. I feel that I went through something like Life Lesson Boot Camp 101 for how to approach every day with a renewed perspective, even if the daily environment was the same as it was the day before. Time will tell how I can reapply this lesson, and I plan to dig deeper into this concept. Somehow, this simple shift to a more minimal structure each day helps me feel the richness of each moment.

Third, I've experienced the beauty of real corners of towns in America, made possible only by driving thousands of miles. Folks in these corners had never heard of me, and likewise, I had never heard of them. Yet that didn't matter. We found true connection in the space of music. We hugged each other's souls and created beauty in those moments. It was an arduous effort for me to do this tour, yet at the same time, it was tremendously rewarding and, of course, beautiful.

I vividly remember the faces, tears, and heartfelt comments from people in those towns. It was as if they'd been waiting for me, even though they didn't realize that they'd been waiting for me. Maybe I made a small difference in their lives. I know they made many in mine.

Indeed I am transformed, probably much more than I could ever describe in words. I am certain that this experience has made me stronger, given me more fuel for life. Yet sometimes I wish life could be easier—and I could have learned all this without going through this rigorous tour. Yet I know—I *know*—that I earned this new knowledge only because I went through every step.

I noticed a daily object in my house became different. It was the same cup that I drank water from in the morning by the window; it was the same piano I have been practicing every day. Yet the feel has changed, perhaps deepened. Then, I realized it is not those things that are changed, but myself, who got to peel off another layer of life to be more grateful—a joy of life experience.

Impromptu in G-flat Major, Op. 90, No. 3, D. 899 by Franz Schubert

Mont by Van ▸

34.

Next-Level Note-Taking

Last week, I was walking on a street in downtown Atlanta after lunching with Karen Thickstun, the former president of the Music Teachers National Association. She stopped in the middle of the conversation and pulled out her phone, saying, "Hold on a second. I can't trust the brain to remember everything." Then, she excused herself to type something on her phone. While waiting for her to finish her note, I thought to myself, *She surely has the note-taking system down.*

Interestingly, I have also observed people's various note-taking methods while attending workshops during conferences. Some didn't seem to make notes at all, some seemed to jot down ideas on a program book or a piece of paper or type on the phone (or they might have been texting someone), and many took pictures of slides with their phones.

When we trace back to some great artists, such as Leonardo da Vinci or even comedians like Jerry Seinfeld, they have often had amazing note-taking systems. Whether paper or digital, they cultivated the habit of capturing passing inspirations or ideas into notes every day.

The author of the resourceful book *Building a Second Brain*, Tiago Forte, explains why we need a method of building what he calls a "second brain" (aka a digital note-taking system) and how to do so efficiently.

I find this concept of having an external storage system for the brain fascinating, because I understand how much space in my brain is required to be creative. With the influx of information we process daily, I can't imagine trying to remember everything. For one thing, I know I won't. More importantly, I don't want to waste my precious working brain simply remembering facts.

> "Your mind is for having ideas, not holding them."
>
> —**DAVID ALLEN,** Author of *Getting Things Done*

I have implemented the following techniques from Forte's book in my own life, which you might also find helpful:

1. Collect information as you live your life. This could be information or inspiration from a YouTube video, highlights from a book, interesting quotes, notes from a meeting, or an interesting website or article. I mostly use *Apple Notes* for this information. I use *Notion* for a project with other people, and for writing my newsletter, I use *Ulysses*. I only use paper notebooks for mindfulness practices. However, to retain knowledge and specific information, I prefer to be able to sort, reorganize, add tags, and search in a digital format.

Forte's book gives us four questions to ask to help decide exactly which nuggets of knowledge are worth keeping:

Does it inspire me?
Is it useful?
Is it personal?
Is it surprising?

2. Organize efficiently for the future. Instead of saving information as general topics, such as health, finances, and so on, put it where you will use it in the future. Create a folder for action-based projects, such as an upcoming workshop, the progress of your health, or a specific personal or professional project. Whenever useful and relevant information comes along, put it in that folder.

Like other conference attendees, I find myself taking photos when I want to remember things. As soon as I take them, I try to move the photos by using the *Adding Photo* function in the *Notes* app under the appropriate project folder. How many times do I later scroll back to those photos of slides? Almost never—unless I move them to a better location right there and then.

Forte suggests that each note or bit of knowledge you capture is like a product you are trying to sell to your future self. Make it easy for your future self to access and use. For this reason, I learned to take one extra minute to reorganize my thoughts or clarify ideas at the time of input so that my future self can remember why I put the information there rather than having to go through it all again so I can figure it out later.

For me, this simple act of organizing for my future self is one of Forte's most eye-opening suggestions. Even though I might have been using this action-based organizational system unconsciously, it has helped me to do so intentionally.

Another interesting idea he suggests is to maintain a gift note-book folder (for Christmas and birthdays) for each person to whom you give gifts. Whenever a new idea or product pops up, put the link or note in that folder. When Christmas or a birthday approaches, you simply open the folder for that person and purchase the item.

Another great way of thinking about this idea is to make prog-ress by slow burns rather than heavy lifting. I have multiple projects that are ongoing concurrently. They can be a public workshop, a

YouTube video, the next podcast episodes, new album ideas, things I want to teach my piano students, or even the muscle-mass progress in my body.

Instead of sitting down one day to start the project from zero to one hundred percent completion, I constantly have all these projects in different stages on the back burner, thanks to the way I've been putting useful information into the right project (folder) over an extended period of time. Then, when the time comes, I can quickly reorganize my ideas into a sharing format: a public talk, writing, recording, and even gift-giving.

I love that Forte emphasizes organizing information, not as a way to collect it but as a tool for future use.

I am curious. What is your methodology? Do you have any note-taking systems that can organize ideas and information as your external brain drives?

No matter what method you use, the most important reminder for the note-taking system is that we are not supposed to remember everything. How often do you forget things as simple as your partner's birthday, the name of your best friend's daughter, or whether or not you shared a certain story with a friend? Instead of heaping more information onto our brain and hoping we remember it, find a method to help ease the burden of remembering. You'll find that this is liberating—and much more trustworthy.

Now, let's make a mental note to look up at the sky this week at least once, and give ourselves a reminder that life is beautiful.

Concert Corner

Finale: Presto from Sonata No. 2 in D Minor, Op. 14 by Sergei Prokofiev

Stay by Van ▶

35.

Will I Make It?

A student raised a hand in the last part of the Q&A during a recent public talk and asked me, "Do you still think about 'Will I make it?'"

Her question caught me off guard. That question surely sounded familiar, as I had asked that myself many times in my youth. For a long time, however, I haven't thought about the question in the context of how she meant it.

In the years of my doctoral studies, I remember asking the following question: *Will I make it sufficiently to have 1) enough money, 2) concerts, and 3) supporters to be able to 4) buy a house and 5) a Steinway piano while also 6) having jobs that are secure, along with everything else I think I need?*

What is interesting is that I clearly remember asking that question of myself, but I don't quite remember putting those numbered items as goals for my life. For me, it felt like an open question that I hoped (or knew) would work out somehow, as long as my intention was in the right place and I worked hard.

In that Q&A, I asked the student a couple of questions back: "Do you know what 'it' is for you? Do you know what makes you happy in life? What is your definition of success—without defining it with numbers or needing approval from others?"

I didn't expect her to be able to answer right then and there. My intention was to give her food for thought, so hopefully, she can ponder these ideas over and over again as she goes through her life.

I grew up under the enormous cultural pressure of the exam system for entering universities in Korea. Studying every waking second and cutting sleep for those tests in your teenage years was expected. I remember literally taking a textbook everywhere, even to the bathroom, to give myself more time to study. Then, when I came to the United States in my early twenties after my undergraduate studies, one of my biggest awakenings was that many people do not work as hard as you think they might.

When I prepared for my exams here, I realized that more than half of my fellow students didn't study as much as I did, so I got relatively better results (even though I still felt underprepared). I gave presentations with maximum effort even though I could have done so with much less preparation. I approached my teaching with care for each student. I prepared everything I did with the utmost intensity: work, teaching, concerts, and studying. Every time I made a total effort to do my best, I felt doors opened unexpectedly, and I experienced new growth in the process.

I learned that by establishing my strong work ethic as my basic principle, financial independence naturally followed without having to actively chase it. Because not many people would work as hard as I did, showing up to do my work consistently was the fastest way to "make it," as far as my early definition of success was concerned.

Surely, when I walked onto the beautiful stage of Carnegie Hall, I felt that I had made it. When my Korean book reached #3 on the bestseller list, I felt I had made it. However, even after whatever great accomplishments I have made, the search for "it" continues to be elusive and never-ending.

That was when I realized that the ongoing search for "Will I make it?" was very much about where my mind was; success depended more on my internal landscape than on what lay outside it.

Now, I still ask that question. This time around, however, my definition of success is more like this: *Will I make it to be in flow with music? Will I make it to be at peace when the storm of life hits me? Will I make it to be happy today? Will I make it to be positive even when I feel discouraged? Will I make it to be in the now in everything I do today? Will I make it to serve and communicate better in my relationships? Will I make it to be vulnerable and open in life? Will I make it to be inspired and inspiring?*

Somehow, when I change my perspective, the never-ending chase of "it" doesn't seem draining anymore. It is such a joy to deepen my relationship with myself and to search for a better version of myself in the process.

Libertango by Astor Piazzolla

Christmas in June by Yeono

HERMGASSE.
ROTHENBURG
OB DER TAUBER.
GERMANY
20240607.
LEON
WINSOR & NEWTON 0.5

36.

Heartfelt Confessions: Life and Loss

I loved my dog, Jenny, when I was growing up. She was a little white poodle, and I have many precious memories of us together—going to the park, sleeping with her in my bed, playing outside, walking, and swimming in the ocean. She was my best friend in my youth, and we did everything together. And she loved my piano playing, keeping me company while I practiced.

One day, when I was out in the yard with her to play with the jump rope, she ran toward a car approaching us. As the car was coming slowly, I thought things would be okay, thinking the car or Jenny would stop in time. I still ran toward her to grab her leash. Then, she thought it was some kind of tag game and started to run faster away from me. My heart pounded.

"Don't do it, Jenny! Don't!"

Then, at that moment, she disappeared under the front of the car but did not come out the back. I stopped in the middle of the road, not sure what to think or what to do. When I walked slowly toward the car and looked underneath it, there was Jenny looking at me. A huge feeling of relief washed over me as I reached my arm under the car and grabbed her little body in my arms.

"Oh, you worried me, Jenny."

But her body was not resisting the way she usually would; it simply draped limply in my arms. I looked at her, and my whole world just turned upside down.

She was dead.

My memories of the period after the accident are vague. I remember that my days were filled with bursts of nonstop crying and that my life had little flavor for a while. That was my first experience with the loss of a loved one.

I have a secret to confess: I haven't had another dog since then. I couldn't dare to have another Jenny and go through that pain again—not to mention that for a long time, I haven't been in the position to have a pet because of my constant travels.

I have another confession to make: More often than not, I fear losing people in my life: my partner, mom, and friends, who are always there for me. I can't imagine what life would be like without their love, shared memories, and support. Just thinking about it, I feel a pain in my chest.

At times, it is challenging for me to balance that fear with abundant love. I know that I need to keep living with the expected pain, appreciating each experience of it fully. That pain is a part of life that I am afraid to go through, yet it's so meaningful and precious to have these amazing people to love in my life. It is surely worth the pain to have them in my life.

I have lost many friends, mentors, and family members in my life, as have you. Every loss hit me in such a way that I felt I was no longer the same person. The pain of loss always seemed to mold me into someone new. I never got over the loss but instead had to learn to live with it.

One thing that has helped me is that I feel the existence of the deceased residing in me as strongly as it did when they were alive. They are right there in my head, or in my heart, everywhere I go, living vividly within me. I still feel the existence of my dog, Jenny, in my heart. Thankfully, whenever I think of Jenny now, a good memory arises first more than the pain of loss: the way we played hide-and-seek, the way she gave me hugs, and the walks we took on a nearby mountain in the early morning.

I believe that we all have abundant, unlimited capacity for giving love. The more I love, the deeper my capacity for love grows, and the more I get back. Whenever I feel the fear of losing someone arising in my mind, I remind myself that one day, I will also be gone. The finiteness of life is beautiful as it is.

Life is short, life is sweet, and life is worth living, even with the painful challenges it throws our way.

Over the weekend, I had a wonderful two-day trip babysitting two adorable family dogs, Wolfie and Connie. As an aunt, spoiling them was the easiest thing in the world, from giving plenty of playtime to cooking chicken for their special meals. At the same time, I sensed that the more I loved them, the more my fear of losing them grew. *Right now, this very moment is all I've got. Don't live in the future, Jeeyoon . . .*

A note to myself:

Choose love over fear. Choose to be positive. Choose to accept. Choose to live fully, now.

Maybe, maybe one day, when I don't travel so much, I will be able to have another pet in my life.

Variations on an Original Theme, Op. 21, No. 1 by Johannes Brahms

Bami and Dessert by MOSLA ▸

greem kim

37.

Both Are Possible

Several years ago, an audience member came up to me after a concert and told me, "You seem to be too normal to be able to perform in the way you do."

I was taken aback by what he had just said. "What do you mean?" I asked.

He continued, "You know, all great artists have some mental issues. Those amazing artists are a little different from us. You seem to be too positive."

I didn't say much then, but his comments lingered with me for a while.

Is being tortured a necessary ingredient for an artist to be amazing?

Last week, I came across a beautifully written op-ed by the pianist Jonathan Biss in *The New York Times* titled "The Myth of the Mad Artist Is Harmful. I Should Know." He talks about how society has fantasized a myth that renders the artist simultaneously superhuman and less than fully human: They have no control over their impulses. They know how to tame lions or conjure infinity, but they cannot be expected to know how to tie their shoelaces. They are totally at home in the world of art; they are utterly out of place in the actual world.

Yes, there are many cases of great artists in history who were terrific at what they did in their art yet also suffered from mental illness. I am sure you could name a few. Robert Schumann, for example, is one of my favorite composers. He suffered from a severe mental illness and ended up being institutionalized at the end of his life.

Does this make his music any more great or less great? Is his mental illness relevant to appreciating the beauty in his music?

Whenever I teach or talk about performance anxiety with my students, most of them are surprised (or relieved) to hear that I, too, have those jittery nerves before a performance. *Of course! We all do!* Many famous performing artists tell stories of hiding backstage, feeling too nervous to perform, and having to be pushed toward the stage by their managers.

We like curtains in front of artists, making them more mysterious. Yet at the same time, we don't like curtains. They block us from seeing them.

We idolize artists and think that they're perfect at what they do. Then, we end up discouraging them from being honest with themselves about many mental issues. This often results in unhealthy relationships between artists and other people and within the artists themselves.

Over the years, I have developed a theory that works for me as a person and as a pianist: Having a healthy mindset equals a happy individual. In the end, healthy, balanced musicians connect better with the music and the audience.

Yes, plenty of artists out there might not have balanced lives, yet they are amazing at what they do. Maybe there is little or no connection between who they are and what they do, but I have striven to find a life that is balanced with positivity. I don't believe that being tortured is a condition for being great at what we do.

We all have struggles in life that make us stronger and, ultimately, make us appreciate life better. On the contrary, having an obnoxiously unhealthy mind and complete disconnection from the real world doesn't help anyone.

As a fellow human being, I sincerely hope that we all find our way out of misery. I don't believe having a mental issue and isolating ourselves in that realm is the only way to express art in the way that certain artists do. Being a balanced person doesn't mean they lose the passion of how they connect with their particular art form.

We can encourage artists to talk openly about their troubles and struggles, as well as ours, and help each other find a peaceful place without shutting down when it comes to such issues.

Being on a stage means that we need to endure the tremendous pressure of the spotlight from outside and within. Music requires the utmost transparency. When music opens the door to the divine world, we escape to another world through that opening. *How can we not lose ourselves in order to be fully in that moment?*

There is a distinction between musicians taking audiences on a journey and musicians making audiences observe the journey from a distance. This is simply a difference in style from musician to musician. Often, many musicians leave the audience behind, making it easier to deal with the pressure onstage. To me, taking a journey with an audience is always more satisfying and healthier, no matter how hard it may be.

I believe, just like with a dream, that there is a time to wake up. Anyone in that divine creative world gets out of the dreamy stage, goes outside in the morning, walks around the neighborhood, chats with strangers about little things, enjoys croissants and cappuccino over good company in the cafe—just being human.

My wish is to not lose that balance as a musician. No matter how amazing it may be in the musical world, I want to keep my foot in the real world and enjoy the mundane small life of being just Jeeyoon.

No, I don't believe that being a tortured artist is a necessary ingredient to greatness. Instead, I believe that being open and connected as a healthy individual is a necessary ingredient to one's happiness on and off the stage. I would always choose to be content first and find my way to express music from there.

To me, both are possible, and life is always better that way.

Concert Corner

Allegro moderato from Sonata in A Major, D. 664 by Franz Schubert

White Wave Village (Yeongdo) by Yuni

흰여울마을

My Ultimate Tool: Sleep

In high school, I remember having two groups of friends before a test: the ones who stayed up as late as possible to study and came to school with a bare minimum of sleep, and the others who didn't change going to sleep no matter how important the test was. I was always the latter. No matter how unprepared I felt for the test, I never replaced sleep with studying.

The night before my doctoral dissertation submission, the night before a piano competition, the night before an important deadline—every hectic moment of my life, even though every minute would count, I stopped and went to sleep.

Looking back, these moments were more physical than mental. I instinctively knew that my primary need to function at my best was to go to bed early and sleep well. I had boundaries. That meant I had to find ways to spend my waking time more efficiently.

That also meant that I didn't party at night in my youth. I was the one sleeping in the corner while everyone else talked and had fun at all-night sleepover parties with my cousins or friends. (My friends called me "Grandma" in my teens.) Maybe I was a party pooper. But I promise that I really tried. Yet no matter what I did, I somehow always found myself falling asleep.

When I went through a difficult time in my life, sleeping was also my salvation. I looked forward to it every day. I felt that I could pause my emotional pain for at least those hours. For the most part, I felt slightly better after sleep. The hard emotions were always easier to deal with in the morning.

I often heard the old school slogan in Korea that encouraged people to sacrifice sleep for doing: "Sleep less; do more!"

I remember feeling guilty for prioritizing sleep. *You could get a lot more done if you slept less, Jeeyoon!*

Thankfully, nowadays, I hear that new scientific studies emphasize the importance of sleep for the brain and mind. Important figures in the field say that one can never replace a good night's sleep. Sleep deprivation is detrimental to long-term physical and mental health. In fact, insufficient sleep appears to be a key lifestyle factor linked to your risk of developing Alzheimer's disease, depression, and even weight gain. Sleep is the single most effective thing we can do to reset our brain and body health each day—Mother Nature's best effort yet at delaying death.

Thank you! Finally!

I never depended on the newest trends in sleep, but it is still great to know that I have been good to myself all along even before I learned the facts. This is what Matthew Walker, a professor of neuroscience and psychology at UC Berkeley, has to say: "A balanced diet and exercise are of vital importance, yes. But we now see sleep as a preeminent force in this health trinity. The physical and mental impairments caused by one night of bad sleep dwarf those caused by an equivalent absence of food or exercise."

No doubt you've heard about the power of having a nighttime routine. Or, perhaps, you have a strict nighttime routine that you keep every night. *Do I have one?* I am not sure. At this point, everything I do is automatic. However, I do many things at night, which might contribute to a night of good sleep.

On an ideal day, I do the following at night:

1. **Wear my Oura ring.** This is preparation for the morning report. I absolutely love to see how I slept through the night. As nerdy as I can be, the everyday data—including my deep and REM sleep time, heart rate variability, resting heart rate, average oxygen saturation, and all the geeky information about my sleep—are very satisfying to know first thing in the morning. Then, I consider that information for my activity for the day. (The ring can also measure my activity during the day, but I wear it only at night because I don't like to wear it when I play the piano.)

2. **Take a hot bath.** A hydrotherapy for me! This is my favorite way to end the day if I can: at least fifteen to twenty minutes of a hot bath with two cups of Epsom salts and three or four drops of various aromatic oils. I rotate the scents depending on my mood.
3. **Wear blue-light-blocking glasses for two or three hours before sleep.** The experts recommend not using the phone or computer for two hours before sleep. Well, that's great advice. Maybe one of these days, I will break this habit. For now, I have a cheating solution. Since not looking at a screen at night is not a simple task, I wear blue-light-blocking glasses. I find that it doesn't affect my sleepiness even when I use a computer or phone. (They say the Kindle screen doesn't affect sleep. That is great!)
4. **Put on mouth tape right before bed.** I have been doing this for over a year. It helps me a lot by guiding me to breathe through my nose at night. (Because of this, I trained myself to breathe more through the nose during the day.) Double score!
5. **Limit caffeine.** My last cup of matcha (or any other caffeinated drink) is five to six hours before going to bed—normally no more after 3 p.m. Yup, I learned this the hard way.
6. **Drink only salty water (electrolytes) before sleep.** I try not to drink water (or any other liquid) at all for the last three hours before bed, but if I want to, I try to drink

only electrolyte salty water, which seems to help me not to wake up at night to go to the bathroom. It is ideal if I can sleep through the night! I generally have about seventy percent success.

7. **Limit late-evening meals.** Having about a four-hour window without eating before sleep is my life habit, because I can't sleep or lie down when my stomach is full. Apparently, this is also very good for your body! No effort is necessary for me to keep this principle. Done!

8. **Sleep at about the same time each night, within a two-hour variable.** I do my best to sleep at the same time as often as possible. But traveling and late concerts can make it tough. You know what, though? I discovered my ultimate weapon: I can sleep on demand. I close my eyes and can fall asleep easily, even at irregular times. Isn't that great? I am very proud of myself for that. It can be quite useful at times.

9. **Save work or study for the morning.** I rarely have a boost of energy to start something new at night. I save it for the morning, because I often feel I can tackle a difficult task at about 9 or 10 o'clock in the morning. If I have energy at night, I usually write what to do tomorrow rather than doing it then. Experts say this is a very good tactic, because mental stimulation can disrupt sleep and make falling asleep harder.

10. **Embrace darkness.** I have blackout curtains or an eye mask when traveling to block all the light.

11. **Wake with the sun.** Lastly, and importantly for me, I do not use an alarm clock. I think this might be one of the most luxurious things in my life. I know my body rhythm. I let my body dictate how long it is appropriate to sleep. If I go to bed on time, I wake up naturally after seven or eight hours of sleep.

What is your night routine? Are you struggling with sleep these days? What is your secret to a good night's sleep?

I hope you get to find a tactic that works for you, and I wish you good sleep tonight!

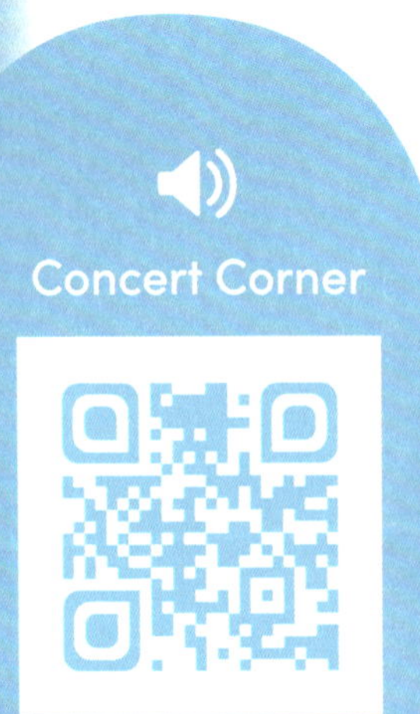

Andante from Sonata in A Major, D. 664
by Franz Schubert

39.

Will You Eat Vegetables Today?

This week, I pondered the idea of "ask, don't tell—the question/behavior effect" from Steven Bartlett in his book *The Diary of a CEO*. He says that if you want to create positive behavior, don't make statements; ask binary yes or no questions. People are more likely to answer yes if it will bring them closer to who they want to be, and once they answer yes, that yes is more likely to come true.

This means, for instance, that a sign that says, "Please recycle" is much less likely to increase its viewers' chances of recycling than a sign that says, "Will you recycle?" Telling yourself, *I will eat vegetables today* is less likely to increase your chances of eating vegetables than asking, *Will you eat vegetables today?*

This week, I've tried this questioning method whenever I felt resistance.

Jeeyoon, will you slow down and focus on sectional practice of this piece? Will you eat a healthy lunch? Will you start a follow-up email draft to that person today? Will you finish this exercise with maximal effort?

According to Bartlett, the question/behavior effect is even more powerful with questions that can only be answered with either yes or no. Starting the question with the word *will* implies ownership and action and causes the question/behavior effect to be even stronger than starting a question with words like *can* or *could*, which imply that the question is about ability rather than action. "Will I go to the gym today?" is more encouraging than "Can I go to the gym today?"

"Will I order healthy food for lunch?" is the way to ask that.

Allow no explanation. Just yes or no.

I like the idea of approaching this question from the second-person perspective, talking to myself as *you*, like a loving life coach would. This method could help a friend or loved one by asking them questions: "Will you eat more healthily?" or "Will you go for that promotion?"

At the end of a piano practice session this week, I noticed I was not focusing as much as I had been at the beginning of the hour. I asked myself, *Jeeyoon, will you finish this practice session with full concentration and keep it in flow?* Interestingly, as soon as I asked that question, I noticed myself correcting my posture to be straight and replying, *Yes!*

The last ten minutes of my practice session were saved, noticed, and, importantly, enjoyable compared with just pushing through them without awareness. I love that a simple tiny life hack like this could make a world of difference at that very moment.

Conversely, one night, I asked myself, *Will you stretch for five minutes?* And I answered, *No*. As they say, *no* is a complete sentence. In fact, I was too tired to push that night. The following day, I was more motivated and inspired to do a full thirty-minute feel-good evening yoga when I had energy. The clarity about how I am doing by asking questions is what I love the most about this method.

Ask questions of your actions, and your actions will answer.

I encourage you to try this method, especially when you feel resistance yet want to direct your actions to be closer to who you want to be.

Please fill in the blank. "Will you ____________________?"

Concert Corner

Allegro from Sonata in A Major, D. 664 by Franz Schubert

The Tapestry of Us by Hye Park

Let Me Experiment

As I write this, I am in New York City attending APAP|NYC, one of the biggest performing arts conferences in the United States and hosted by the Association of Performing Arts Professionals. I interact with fellow artists, agents, and presenters worldwide, sharing music and creating opportunities for future concert engagements. This year, they say there are more than 2,800 attendees, one of the largest crowds ever. The conference hotel is sold out. People are buzzing around and interacting everywhere you turn. It's loud, lively, overwhelming, and energizing all at the same time. They seem more than ready to resume creating art for the world after a long pause during the pandemic.

I was supposed to attend an opening-night reception dinner tonight, where one mingles with hundreds of people passing by, introducing each other and networking. I diligently prepared my thirty-second elevator speech I'd use to introduce myself. But then, at the last minute, I decided to hide in my hotel room and have a quiet evening alone. As much as I feel bad about missing out on a potential opportunity to create a great connection, I don't feel bad about knowing my limits. I am getting better at gauging a fine line between what I can do and what I will do instead for a healthy balance. In the next four days, I will have plenty of time to connect with people, drawing on my extroverted side while putting on hold my introverted inclination.

Standing in front of my booth in the exhibit hall the next day, someone glanced back and forth at my face and then behind me at the enlarged poster of me playing piano and asked, "Do you have an agent?"

To make a long story short, the answer is no. But to make a short story long, yes, I do. I created my own booking agent company five years ago called Namus Classics, and I am the CEO and the sole artist in the company. *Namu* means "tree" in Korean; I added an *s* at the end to create the meaning of plural "trees" and then added *Classics*. I hired a manager, a PR agent, a graphic designer, and people for other work that needs to be done project by project. I travel to performing arts conferences throughout the year to represent myself. I manage my schedule, create funding, and scope out what works and what doesn't for each project. (Exclusively for Korea, though, I have a contract with a classical music agency.)

I find that being my own agent is harder than I anticipated. Where do you even start after being fresh out of school? It requires a high level of marketing, branding, planning, organizing, social skills, and networking, which is a daunting task for one person. None of the curricula in my higher education taught me about these hidden aspects of being an artist in this era. I had to learn from trial and error. Yes, it is a lot of work, but it is liberating at the same time to create a life path and take action on your own terms. I never wait for opportunities to come to me. I go and get them.

One of the lessons I've learned from being my own agent is that whenever I am unsure about things, I say that it is an experiment: *I am experimenting with this to see whether it might work* or *I don't know whether this feels right yet, so let me experiment with it.*

When I put things into an experimenting category, it seems okay to accept the potential negatives and makes it easier to embrace them. It is all about trying out options and experiencing the results as they come. I don't have to label anything or judge something as good or bad; I simply need to let go and let things unfold.

An example of this is the way I approached my music education. Before I decided to apply for graduate school, I experimented with living in both Germany and the United States. I knew those two countries would offer the kind of musical education I needed. I didn't know which country would be a better fit for me, so I had to experience both of them fully before making that life-changing decision. So during my two summer breaks in my undergraduate years, I spent a full six weeks living like a local in two small cities: Freiburg in Germany one summer and Columbia in South Carolina in another.

I landed in Columbia because I'd been accepted as a language exchange student from my university in South Korea for six weeks with a full scholarship. I immersed myself in the southern culture of America as well as university life, spending many hours at the campus of the University of South Carolina. As a southern girl myself, born and raised in the southern city of Pusan in South Korea, I found that the warmth of South Carolina felt like a home away from home. I didn't know back then that within the United States, there were huge cultural differences between the cities.

Although the sophisticated, rich classical music scene in Freiburg impressed me greatly, I felt like a stranger. No matter how many weeks or months I spent in this beautiful city, I couldn't help but sense that I would feel like oil on top of water. There was something very foreign about the culture there for me.

Nonetheless, it was interesting for me to feel the subtle and, at other times, the big cultural nuances of each country by living there. There was something very valuable about me jumping into the scene as an experiment rather than gathering information about different cultures or reading about them from the outside. There was no regret or *what if?* or *what could this be like?* when the time came to choose between the two pathways. In the end, when I chose to move to the United States for my education, it was both intuitive and easy to listen to my inner voice after that rich experimentation.

This week at this conference, I will be experimenting with many things: I will experiment with how I interact with new people. I will experiment with how I like being my own agent all over again. I will experiment with talking to strangers.

Maybe life is all about experiments.

The Soul of Porto by Yuni

“People often ask me what is the most effective technique for transforming their life. It is a little embarrassing that after years and years of research and experimentation, I have to say that the best answer is—just be a little kinder.”

—ALDOUS HUXLEY, PHILOSOPHER

THE FIFTH MOVEMENT: Presto

41.

Dancing with the Lion: Turning Anxiety into Art

The light is on. The noise of enthusiastic crowds fills the space. It is finally time to perform.

I felt that familiar sensation of butterflies in my stomach when I sat in the Staples Center stadium in Los Angeles—only it wasn't for me. It was for the professional basketball players who were about to take the floor in an NBA game between the Los Angeles Lakers and the Boston Celtics.

Though I was not performing that night, I couldn't help noticing the pressure the players must have been feeling in those moments. Some seemed to manage to get into the flow throughout the game while others seemed to be a bit beaten up by their mind battles, looking stressed every time they had to stop and shoot free throws.

You might not be a pianist or professional basketball player who performs in front of hundreds or thousands of people. Still, no matter what we're doing or when we're doing it, we've all known how it feels to be extremely nervous before a performance.

How do you prepare for a performance? How do you deal with performance anxiety?

I wish there were a magical pill to fix it all. There is a myth among musicians that eating bananas before the performance helps calm one's nerves. Many of my musician friends swear by this theory. However, no matter how many bananas you consume before a performance, it won't solve the fundamental challenge of the mind game.

Over the years, I've discovered that many methods used by athletes can be effective for the performing arts—and certain tools probably saved my career. My secret has been experimenting with as many methods as possible over a long time and maintaining a certain crucial mind (mental) practice regularly, even turning that practice into a daily discipline as the day of the performance drew closer.

This isn't a light topic that I can cover within the scope of this essay. Still, I will share my top three daily mind practices that I do before a performance.

First, embrace the power of positive visualization. I visualize detailed positive performance scenarios from the moment I wake up: the scents, feelings, touches, sounds, and scenes. I write out at least one such scenario; then, I read it daily.

Here is one little example of me being in the greenroom right before the performance: I hear chattering noises coming from the audience in the main hall. They are here to enjoy this wonderful experience with me. I think, *How privileged I am to get to share music with them!* I focus on breathing while moving my body slowly on my yoga mat. The smell of the concrete building and the rubber scent from the yoga mat create a strange harmony of the current moment. These thirty minutes before the performance don't exist only for my performance but also for this very moment of my life. *Don't live in the future, Jeeyoon. You have prepared well up to this moment. All work is done. Now, smile and enjoy this moment. Let the music carry you. Be in this moment. Feel the gratitude for this experience. Every experience is worth having. Let it go. I feel ready and excited.*

You can create this in whatever way you want and own it by repeating this positive scenario. (Faking it till you make it will work in your favor.) One of the most important aspects of this practice is to create (think of) yourself as the most grateful and positive person in this world, as well as creating (imagining) the warmest and most enthusiastic audience. Even if you are not a performer, you can apply this method in other fields of your life. Imagine a difficult conversation you are about to have with your parents or spouse; you can still practice visualizing the most positive scenario of being yourself in a new or scary environment.

I find that by creating this optimal scenario beforehand, I get to develop a positive mindset. To me, having a positive mindset when I need it the most was the hardest to execute, much more difficult than how to play a difficult piano repertoire in front of big crowds. Treat this technique like a daily mind muscle exercise, and start doing it today. Your future self will thank you for it.

Second, embrace the power of breathing through the nose. Whether you are actively meditating, walking around the neighborhood, or surfing, breathe deeply in and out through the nose. I often put my hand on my belly to feel my nervous system settle down and slow down my breathing rhythm consciously. I say a mantra or short positive word as I breathe, count my breathing, or simply am aware of breathing. My favorite this week is to say *breathe in love* as I inhale and *breathe out joy* as I exhale. I don't say it out loud; I merely imagine those phrases.

I do this as often as possible whenever and wherever I can. Other variations are *breathe in warmth; breathe out love* and *breathe in calm; breathe out peace.* Waiting in line? No problem—it's the perfect time to do this breathing work.

Third, embrace the power of repeated performance. The legendary swimmer Michael Phelps practiced racing every single day as part of training since his youth. When you always practice performing, whether in front of several people or on an Olympic stage, the day you perform becomes a part of your system—just another day in the pool.

I often give my piano students the solid advice to "do seven performances before the actual performance" as a minimal requirement. If performance is your daily activity, there is no way that your body will react in a way that's extremely out of character.

Do trial-run performances often. Get friends and family to be your audience. Repeat this over and over. At the very least, you will be accustomed to having this lion—your performance anxiety—appearing next to you at the time of the performance. Then, I promise that you will (soon) also learn that you can tame the lion, little by little.

The beauty of feeling performance nerves is that you will realize that the lion is your friend, who helps you perform your best. We do need a little dose of performance nerves to heighten our senses to the most sensitive stages of our mind and body. Often, to me (and many performing artists agree), the best performance is not when we are totally relaxed in our living room or performing alone wearing our pajamas but performing in front of someone, a body of people, with the lion next to us, keeping us company. After all, the right amount of performance nerves is helpful and is exactly what we need for optimal presentation. Once you accept this notion, you will find that the lion ends up *giving* you energy rather than taking it away. You don't need to combat this lion (performance nerves); you need to dance with him. Look for the lion if he is not there. You need him!

Like many performing artists, I also wished I could say one day, "I don't feel nervous when I perform anymore." However, even after over twenty years of performing, that day has not come, and I know it never will.

One of the bits of wisdom I've gained from every stage I've performed on is that I am always secure and grounded, regardless of how I feel. I sometimes feel like I am standing on a bungee jumping dock, wondering whether the rope attached to my body will actually hold me as I fall.

I've learned that the feeling of butterflies in my stomach is a rather healthy and good sign that I am fully alive and open to receiving what life gives me in that very moment. This vulnerability allows me to connect deeper with myself, with the music, and with my audiences.

As we all do, I have experienced many levels of vulnerability onstage and elsewhere in life: the moment before a difficult conversation, the first meeting with a stranger in a conference room, the fear of losing people I love, losing a job, admitting that I made a mistake, fear of others' judgment, waiting for a doctor's call—the list goes on. Whenever I face anything that seems bigger than I can grasp, I try to take a deep breath and find my inner voice, which is seated deep inside me, guiding me wisely.

The moment before I went on the stage at my last concert, I recited these sentences to myself: *I am a vessel of love, and I am loved. I am transparent and free from negativity. I am grounded and safe. What a joy to give and receive music! The only thing I need to do right now is be here at this very moment. Let it go. Let everything go, including wishes. Just courageously be yourself. Trust that you are enough.*

Whenever you feel vulnerable, I hope that you also believe that vulnerability is a positive sign that we are alive. It presents an opportunity to grow and learn how to let it go. I find that courage is nothing fancy. It's just being able to sit with a sense of vulnerability and quietly seek the wisdom within.

I've learned from daily mind practice for my performance nerves that with consistent, persistent practice, this tricky mind game gets easier. Treat it like dust that settles in your mind daily; the more actively you embrace it and work on it, the more grounded you will feel. Ultimately, you can be fully yourself—with performance nerves tagging along.

Concert Corner

Promenade from *Pictures at an Exhibition* by Modest Mussorgsky

Embraced by Autumn by Van

42.

With a Thankful Heart

Sitting in an airport in Denver, I am waiting for my flight to San Diego for a five-day break for Thanksgiving. I just finished my eleventh concert this month, covering at least 3,300 miles on the road (which is more than the drive from New York City to Los Angeles by 500 miles) and going through a snowy winter wonderland here near the Rocky Mountains. I have more concerts on this tour after Thanksgiving break, but I made it through the toughest part and am happy to have a moment to take a deep breath.

Each concert was unique. Each town had a different vibe. Each piano had a different sound, character, and various shortcomings and strengths—not to mention brand and size. I stayed in a different room every night. All I could do in that ever-changing environment was to stay focused and true to the meaning of what I do.

When I finally got a moment to sit in this airport alone, I had an overwhelming rush of emotions coming to me, and I cried for a while. The tears weren't of sadness or joy. They were of relief from all that I had held on to. I survived it. Not only did I do it, I did it well and with grace.

You did it, Jeeyoon. Well done . . .

I know from the bottom of my heart that I couldn't have done these concerts without my lifelong friend Joseph Bercovici, who stepped in from Indianapolis as the road manager for the first half of the tour. He helped me by driving the rental minivan, cooking every meal, packing lunch boxes (we didn't go to a single restaurant; can you believe that?), loading and unloading gear, providing tech assistance for the concert, taking videos and photos, selling CDs, and basically everything else needed to help the process go smoothly—besides performing.

Joseph is an advanced piano player and has also worked as a chef and professional baker. He is a poet who loves reading good English literature. I own several beautiful pieces of his black-and-white nature photography, which is framed on a wall in my house. Because of his artistic and intelligent mind, the two of us shared hours of car rides (sometimes a whole day of driving) with nonstop conversations about topics—which we never ran out of. I mean, how perfect is that combination as a road manager?

In his car, he brought his cast iron pan, a loaf of homemade sourdough bread, spices, tools to fix a car on the road, and other cookware, including a professional cooking knife. His life motto is "to find creative solutions for everyday life challenges." He found a practice spot for me to keep my fingers warmed up in every new town, from local churches to the houses of piano teachers, between my performance schedules. For each town, he took care to find the best lodging in advance. Many times, there weren't any hotels nearby, and in those cases, local houses via Airbnb were way better options than motels.

Every accommodation we arrived at had a few surprises. One house we stayed at in North Dakota had a deer head hanging above my bed, and chickens were running loose in the yard. We played a game of predicting the owner's personality and career based on their book collections. Our challenges for each concert became comic relief—things we will joke about for a long time. We laughed and shared the pain as well as the victories. From the bottom of my heart, I thank you, Joseph!

One of the things I've noticed on this tour is the fact that people find pronouncing my name very difficult. I often explain the pronunciation by asking people to say the month of June with a Southern accent, which sounds fine enough to my ear. But many people found it almost impossible to say my name even with that trick and were often stressed about it when they introduced me to the audience at the beginning of the concert.

One presenter got a particularly long coaching session with me in the greenroom. He called me "Sheeyoon" at first, so I kindly corrected him that it is not "Shee" but "Jee." He was shocked to learn that he had been practicing my name wrong all week and thankful to have figured it out before the concert.

Minutes later, as I waited behind the curtain for the concert to begin, I heard this man pronounce my name correctly several times as he introduced me. *Good!* I thought. *He figured out how to say my name in the end.* Then, in a final flourish, he announced with great enthusiasm, "Now, without further ado, let us welcome the pianist, Sheeyoon—[a long pause]—JEE!"

I almost died of laughter behind the curtain, but I held it together and walked on the stage. He realized that he had pronounced my name wrong, which led to an even bigger mistake.

Ever since that event, whenever I came to our living room in the morning, Joseph announced with great energy, "Here comes the greatest pianist, Sheeyoon Jeeeee!" In fact, we decided that the official name of the tour should now be "Sheeyoon Jee!"

I am thankful that I have this Thanksgiving break to come down to earth, regenerate, and take a deep breath to process what I have done and where I have been. I am thankful for each and every concert that I gave this month. I am transforming and absorbing everything that life has to offer me, no matter how my name is pronounced.

"The Gnome" from *Pictures at an Exhibition* by Modest Mussorgsky

Going Home by Yuni

43.

Clarity of the Mind

August is almost over. All of a sudden, I am having a sense of urgency that everything is about to start, but I am not quite ready. My mind wants to wander off a bit longer in the spacious, relaxed summer mood. And then I noticed that the stores in town have already changed their displays to a fall theme, and the new academic year is about to start with full force. Uh-oh, I definitely feel behind.

I used to feel the new beginning of the year in January, but ever since I've lived in the United States and worked in the academic and art seasonal calendar, it feels more like September is the first month of the year. It is funny how the culture changes our perception of time.

In a typical season, I would fly out of town at least twice a month. This has gradually increased over the years. You might think that by this point, I am a master of packing. On the contrary! No matter how much I plan and simplify my packing to the most essential items, I am amazed by the fact that I still carry huge suitcases with just-in-case items that end up not being used. (Thank God I do not travel with a piano.)

At the same time, it is interesting to me that every time I return—after any trip away from home, whether for work or leisure—I have a different perspective on my daily life. I ask or think to myself:

Do I really need this?

If I could live out of two suitcases for a month, maybe I don't need these clothes.

Maybe I should have more of a staycation in my city, exploring it like a curious tourist.

Detoxing from the convenience of the modern world was refreshing. I would like to spend less time on devices now.

Just like Melissa Kirsch writes in a recent *New York Times* article titled "The Post-Vacation Clarity," "I keep thinking about the wise friend who told me that everything you buy makes everything you own less valuable. . . . This change in perspective, I think, . . . is the most transformative possibility of vacation. . . . You return determined to maintain some of that lightness."

I love the part that you can keep that "lightness" after your return. Everything indeed seems a bit easier and lighter after time away from our routines. It is transformative and gives me a valuable new perspective on life.

It doesn't have to be a fancy, exotic vacation to give you that new perspective. A hike in your area or a long walk or a day trip might be just enough. I am constantly searching for balance, clarity, and peace in my life. One moment, I seem to have it; another moment, I am completely out of balance again. Ah, what a hard life lesson that is to acquire!

Here are three things I've done this week in order to declutter my mind and environment:

1. Clean the house before I start the day. It can be making the bed, putting things in their places, and having nothing on the kitchen counter. (This last one is always harder than I think.)
2. Give away at least five pieces of clothes or other things that I didn't use this past year, and drop them off at a local donation center. And keep on constant lookout for unloved and/or unused items in my space.
3. Identify the most difficult task that I have been avoiding, write it on paper, put it on the desk, and decide when I will tackle it. Then, follow through at the scheduled time.

As simple as these steps may seem, I feel they make a difference in my mind. In my experience, thinking about something without taking action has created the most difficult sense of mental stuckness. Clearing my space has always been my conscious first step into the gray mental fog that I have been avoiding.

Feeling behind? Or are you procrastinating a difficult task? Maybe cleaning your room will be a step closer to decluttering your mind, getting unstuck, and accomplishing your goals.

Promenade and "Il Vecchio Castello" ("The Old Castle") from *Pictures at an Exhibition* by Modest Mussorgsky

The Flowers Picked from the Garden by MOSLA

Progress, Not Perfection: The Gift of Practice

I enjoy deciding on a New Year's resolution at the end of every year. I don't always get to realize these resolutions, but I love the idea of resetting my intentions yearly once again. I ask myself, *Is there any area of my life to which I need to pay more attention? Do my actions reflect what I am passionate about and my principles in life?*

When I consider New Year's resolutions, I often think of a big category in life, such as health, relationships, career, finances, spirituality, and so on, like a wheel of life. Then, I try to find a system that I can use to improve daily within any category that seems weaker than the others. For example, one year, I decided to think about three different things that I am grateful for when I first wake up and make a mental list as I lay in bed, which eventually became a daily ritual ever since that year. I always have several new sets of piano repertoires that I want to tackle in the new year as well.

However, despite my initial enthusiasm, whenever I learn a new piece of music, I am still amazed at how long it takes to learn a piece to be ready to perform it. I mean not simply to the point that I am playing the right notes from memory but playing at the level of total freedom that I can transcend through music. Even then, the day I can say I have conquered the piece never comes. After many successful public performances, the music continually evolves, changing daily, as do I. Sometimes, it feels like a betrayal when the section I thought I knew securely suddenly doesn't go as I thought it would onstage.

The legendary cellist János Starker practiced Bach's Cello Suites every single day, even when he was in his nineties. He performed the Suites hundreds, if not thousands, of times throughout his life. People asked him why he kept practicing the piece he knew better than anyone in this world. His answer was, "I can feel I am making progress."

He was on to something. The mindset of a master is that one can never master mastery. As frustrating as it can sometimes be, it is joyous to feel a small pinch of success from the everyday practice of getting better. Starker's daily practice was not about winning a competition or public performances but about the intrinsic rewards of making progress. The world got to listen to his wonderful performance as a gift and the outcome of his desire to share.

Seth Godin says in his book *The Practice*, "The practice is not the means to the output, the practice *is* the output, because the practice is all we can control."

He adds, "Creativity doesn't repeat itself. However, the creative journey still follows a pattern. It is a practice of growth and connection, of service, and daring. It's also a practice of selflessness and ego in an endless dance. The practice exists for writers and leaders and for teachers and painters. It's grounded in the real world, a process that takes us where we hope to go."

I love that creativity results from the desire to find a new truth, solve an old problem, or serve someone else. Creativity is a choice, not a bolt of lightning from somewhere else.

Whenever I feel too drained to do my work, I remind myself to focus on being in the never-ending process. It is a persistent, step-by-step approach that we pursue for its own sake and not because we want anything guaranteed in return.

I ask myself, *Am I helping someone? Am I in the process of creating in the service of the better?* Then, I'll need to reframe my thinking:

I haven't reached my goals (so far).

I am not as good at my skill as I want to be (not yet).

I am struggling to find the courage to create (so far).

This is wonderful! Something isn't there when I want it, but then it is. Persistent and consistent efforts over time can yield results. *So far* and *not yet* are the stepping stones of every successful journey.

Starker might still be practicing his Bach Cello Suites every morning if he were still alive, telling himself, *I am not there yet.*

So now, it is your turn. When you make a new plan for your life, try to consider these five elements of the practice of life:

1. **Growth:** What can I do to learn and grow more this year?
2. **Connection:** What can I do to create more meaningful connections and relationships with others?
3. **Service:** What can I do in the service of helping other people and this world?
4. **Daring:** How can I go on a journey with my eyes wide open, trusting the process and myself to create my best contribution?
5. **Letting go:** Selflessness and ego are in an endless dance. How can I let go of myself more?

I hope you get to enjoy the *not yet* journey of finding endless joy in your daily life. Writing a book? Training for a marathon? Preparing a feast for a family gathering? Remember that the daily process for reaching what seems to be a clear end goal is still one of the most rewarding aspects of the journey itself. Don't forget to pause and acknowledge these joyous moments of life.

Keep practicing!

Concert Corner

Promenade and "Tuileries" ("Children's Quarrel After Games")
from *Pictures at an Exhibition* by Modest Mussorgsky

Adorable Couple
by Nakseo Jaengi Kim

Adorable couple

낙서쟁이 김선생

I Could Be Wrong . . .

Several months ago, my dentist asked me at my regular checkup whether I ground my teeth at night. I said, "No. Absolutely not."

She tilted her head and screened my teeth again, saying that there was a sign of grinding or biting down hard. She added, "Let's wait and see at your next visit, but why don't we make a mold for a retainer just in case you do?"

I agreed to it but thought that she was being overly cautious because I knew I didn't grind my teeth at night.

Me? No way! Only someone like my brother does that, who snores like bombs dropping into the Pacific Ocean, making creative percussive music with his mouth while he sleeps. I dare you to fall asleep with him next to you! (I never could. I needed at least one room or two walls of separation between us.)

Then, one night, I woke up from a nightmare in the middle of the night. With a sigh of relief that it was just a dream, I opened my eyes. That was it—the moment I noticed something: I was clenching my jaw. Very hard. It was as if I had to hold on to a piece of paper with my teeth to keep from dropping it.

I was lying in bed in shock, not because I was clenching my jaw but for the fact that I could be that wrong with my judgment about myself. I was sure that I was not a person who clenched or ground her teeth.

When did it start? How could I not know about it for this long?

On the next visit to the dentist, I confessed that I indeed clenched my jaw at night and thanked her for pointing me in the right direction. I said that I wasn't sure when it started or how long I had been doing it, but now I knew that I did. She interestingly commented that more than eighty percent of her patients who need a retainer at night go through the same denial. In fact, lots of people still refuse to wear anything to protect their teeth because they don't believe that they clench or grind their teeth, even with clear evidence! Oh, wow! Maybe it might take another year or decades for them to realize the truth.

This experience reminded me of other occasions when I had a similar epiphany in my life—the moment when I woke up from a belief to a hard reality. That moment, everything seemed upside down as I finally faced a truth that I couldn't even imagine could possibly be true.

One of the lessons I've learned from those experiences is that now, I often say to myself, *I could be wrong . . .* That sentence helps my thinking to be flexible and open to being changed by other ideas. And it also helps me to be ready to rebuild the idea from zero. As long as my way of thinking stays open, I can accept the counterargument to learn and grow.

I could be wrong, but I believe . . .

I could be wrong, but I think . . .

To me, these sentences are not a sign of weakness but the attitude of a learner. They are part of a humble yet peaceful conversation with myself.

After being broken down by the many layers of hard shells around me, I finally started to learn the value of the vulnerability of the human mind.

"When it challenges your intelligence, lean in more. When it makes you feel stupid, lean in more. Leaning out will leave you behind. Don't block people that you don't agree with; follow more of them. Don't run from ideas that make you uncomfortable; run towards them."

—STEVEN BARTLETT

How might you use the statement, "I could be wrong . . ."?

Concert Corner

"Bydło" ("The Ox Cart") from *Pictures at an Exhibition*
by Modest Mussorgsky

Hello, Sweet Summer by Hye Park

46.

I Speak Spanish (Kind of . . .)

When I arrived in San Diego, one of the first things I noticed was the bilingual characteristics of the city, being so close to Mexico. I saw many signs in Spanish and heard Spanish-speaking people everywhere. For the first time, I realized that *San Diego* meant "Saint Diego" in Spanish! Duh, that makes sense!

I thought that if I could learn English proficiently enough as my second language, maybe I could figure out Spanish, too.

Unlike my ambitious motivation, I had a slow start. I was frustrated that I had no idea what they were discussing over a Spanish-speaking podcast I played in the background. (I thought that listening to Spanish in the background as a language-immersion method would magically make me a Spanish speaker.) I glanced through several grammar books to build a structure without worrying about the details or memorizing any of them. It was a valid approach, but it was not enough.

I memorized several useful phrases and tried to use them at the local farmer's market. They somehow always answered me in broken English while they spoke fluent Spanish. "No," I said. "Please speak Spanish to me!" I must have sounded very foreign, not to mention that they probably noticed my level-zero Spanish.

After getting lost alone in a Spanish-learning world for several months, I was getting tired of trying hard and getting nothing in return.

In the midst of disappointment, I asked myself, *Why do you want to learn Spanish?* I narrowed it down to three reasons:

1. I love the challenge of a new language and the way it stimulates my brain. That challenge (weirdly) makes me happy.
2. I want to give a concert in a Spanish-speaking country one day, talking on the stage and conversing with the audience afterward—not memorized phrases but a real conversation in Spanish.
3. I love gaining a deeper understanding of cultures by learning their languages.

After analyzing my reasons, I noticed that each one was about personal growth and connection.

One of the best things I did at that time was find an instructor to whom I could talk and who would give me some structure. That is when I met my teacher Marco Fierro from Chile, through the language learning website *italki*. Still to this day, after more than three years, we meet on Zoom almost weekly and talk about life—in Spanish. His podcast *Latin ELE* has also been a great addition to my studies.

I now speak Spanish okay. Traveling through Spanish-speaking countries shouldn't be a problem for me. Can I discuss politics or difficult subjects? Probably not (yet).

This morning, I learned a new phrase, *la funda de edredón*, meaning "duvet cover." With a big sigh over the thousands of words I still have to learn, I was here again this morning, jotting those new words into my notebook and repeating them out loud.

One of the interesting statistics my instructor, Marco, told me was that despite years of teaching Spanish in his private class and among his podcast listeners, the majority are still beginners, and few are intermediates.

I asked what happened to those beginners: "Don't they become intermediate at some point?"

Apparently, not always. Just like gym memberships in January skyrocket and then slowly go down over the year, learning a new language in the long term is a big task. Students start with enthusiasm but quit for one reason or another soon afterward.

I might not be the most fluent Spanish speaker, but I am proud that I haven't stopped. I realize that consistency is harder than learning the language for some people.

What is the key to keeping going for me? It is to create a system that works, such as learning a new word every day or scheduling a conversation with a teacher and sticking to it—something small that I'm able to manage consistently. I feel the good sensation of learning something new at each lesson and not comparing my progress to that of others. The journey is there for me and only for me. I don't need to prove anything.

Last week, I had an appliance delivered to my house. A couple of guys talked to each other in Spanish, and I understood what they were talking about. (*Hooray!*) I didn't remark, as I didn't want to disturb their work, but as they were leaving, I said, "Muchas gracias por su ayuda" ("Thank you very much for your help"). They probably thought that I had memorized the phrase and it was all I knew in Spanish. No matter. They responded enthusiastically, "Thank you!"

To me, understanding another language is like entering a new realm that I haven't yet experienced. From Chile to Colombia to Spain, just because they speak Spanish doesn't mean they share the same culture. Those differences between Spanish-speaking countries (which are a lot more countries than I originally realized) were not subtle anymore once I could get past the language barrier and draw closer to the people in that region.

Not experiencing other cultures is a bit like the difference between watching a movie in black and white versus in full high-definition color. Until you see a better version, you don't know what you are missing. I believe no matter how advanced our technology becomes—with artificial intelligence or translation devices—we'll never be able to replace the joy of deeper connection between humans that comes with simply speaking the same language.

The real joy, the real connection, truly comes from within.

Concert Corner

Promenade and "Ballet of the Unhatched Chicks" from
Pictures at an Exhibition by Modest Mussorgsky

A Cozy Winter by Hye Park

Your Unique Brand of Magic

Last month was pretty hectic for me because I gave many concerts in a relatively short time. It was wonderful to be back onstage to share music with live audiences again, yet I was reminded how difficult it is to be a performing artist, being vulnerable onstage regardless of how much I practice or prepare.

I heard a story that even the legendary pianist Vladimir Horowitz needed to be kicked out to the stage every time he gave a concert, as he would hesitate because of his jittery nerves. Really? Horowitz—one of the best pianists in history?

It's true: Regardless of one's proficiency, this field of the performing arts does not always get easier over time.

Last month, one of my concerts was a three-day series in

which the repertoire of each concert did not change. I certainly and hopefully wished that each performance would get easier after completing a victorious one the day before.

The reality was far beyond what I had hoped: Each concert felt completely new, raw, and vulnerable all over again. Each one was a new day, a different audience, a different feeling, and even a different me at the piano. If I were a tour guide on the Appalachian Trail, after triumphantly completing the rigorous trek from Georgia all the way to Maine, I'd feel as though the very next day, I'd somehow been pulled back to Georgia to start all over again.

In the morning after each concert, I lay in bed thinking, *Do I have the courage to walk this trail again?*

But the moment I started playing the next concert, I was somehow back to a life in which my senses were heightened, finding new beauty and treasure in each corner and being joyous that I could share the music despite the fear and doubt inside me. I was alive—and on the trail once again.

After a solo concert in Encinitas, California, a member of the audience came to me in tears, grasping my hand tightly and sharing that the hour of that concert would be something she would never forget, and she believed it would give her energy every time she thought about it and relived it. And she thanked me for that gift. In that very moment, I had been actually beating myself up a bit about having made this and that mistake, thinking how I could make some sections of the music better next time and collecting data for what I needed to practice later.

On that day, I had a quiet moment with myself and reminded myself of this mantra, shared by Amie McNee; it's the mantra that I want to live with, the mantra that I need to keep reminding myself of: "Artists are not like athletes. We cannot win gold. We cannot 'beat' other creatives. We cannot come first. Sport is objective. Our craft is subjective. Creating to 'be the best' is a waste of energy. Instead, create to connect to the people who need you, because they're out there. Create in your way, because there is no right way. Take the pressure off, and focus on your unique brand of magic."

What is your unique brand of magic? Just remember: That's the magic that belongs only to you.

Concert Corner

"Samuel Goldenberg and Schmuÿle" from
Pictures at an Exhibition by Modest Mussorgsky

I Like Yellow by J RYU

48.

Courage Found on a Bicycle

Last week, I went to New York City to record my next album, 시음 */si-úm/* (a made-up phrase that means "poetry–music"). After many delays and cancellations due to the pandemic of 2020, I was finally able to make this trip. Although New York was definitely different and included many restrictions related to the pandemic, it was still great to feel its positive energy. It takes patience, but we hope to get some normalcy back into our lives.

After four days of intense work in a recording studio, I finally took a free day to relax, so I decided to walk outside, enjoy the beautiful spring weather, and absorb the city. I noticed many cyclists on the roads. Some had serious looks on their faces as if they were in a hurry to get from A to B—typical busy New Yorkers. Others seemed to just enjoy cycling for leisure.

I thought with excitement, *This could be fun! Maybe I should make bicycle riding my new thing to try today.* There is a network called City Bike that lets you grab a bike, go for a ride, and then park the bike in any of the hundreds of spots in the city. So I decided to try it, which was an easy decision. As I walked to the bikes, I noticed new thoughts arising: *What if I have an accident?* (A valid concern.) *I don't know what I'm doing with the City Bike system. How do I start? Maybe it is just easier to walk, which I normally do and know exactly how to do.* (Avoiding trying something unfamiliar.) *The system is complicated and unfamiliar; I just want to give up.* (Thinking negatively.)

I stood in front of the bikes, listening to the battle in my head. After a while, I got to a point where I could be more neutral about my arising negative thoughts. I felt that I *had to* fight against my negativity and rise above it. Yes, it was just a bike—but it was more than that. It was me wanting to avoid unfamiliarity and new territory that I had never explored.

So I downloaded an app (which took a while), registered (which I wasn't sure would be worth it yet), chose a payment option, and for five minutes read the instructions on what to do. I carefully observed and copied what others did, such as taking a picture of the QR code to unlock their bikes. I felt excitement growing. *You are taking action. Keep it up!* I unlocked a bike, adjusted the seat, and decided to go to the Chelsea Market, which seemed like a fun new place to see. I sat on the bike, took a deep breath, and hit the road.

Once I realized that it was so much safer than I anticipated because bike lanes were mostly separated from roads for cars, I felt relief. Those traffic jams in New York also made me feel that going around on a bike was ten times faster. I was wearing fancy clothes (which were not meant for cycling), but I didn't care. With the spring breeze on my face, I felt freedom, a sense of accomplishment, and joy, which I would have missed if I hadn't taken that first step away from my initial resistance.

I realize that I encounter these obstacles of thought much more often in daily life. It may not be as big as a new adventure like riding a bike in New York City; instead, it's daily small things like choosing a route to go to the grocery store. New things always seem to be complicated. My mind craves to do the things I already know and am familiar—and comfortable—with and to avoid new challenges. Yet I also learned that the joy that comes from overcoming any resistance nurtures our minds and expands our capacity to accept new ideas.

I'm sure I am not alone in this discovery. I'm curious about your experience with this type of resistance and how you feel after taking the first step. I hope that we will get stronger by exercising the muscle of a flexible mindset more in our daily lives, which comes about only as we take more first steps into the unknown.

Concert Corner

Promenade from *Pictures at an Exhibition* by Modest Mussorgsky

Between the City and Stillness by Mclalan

49.

Change from *Have to* to *Get to*

For the last four weeks, my life has been completely taken over by translating my book *Whenever You're Ready* into Korean, which is scheduled to be published in Korea this summer through Dasan Book Publishing. When I first spoke with the Korean publisher, they told me a professional translator was working on my book already, because that's the usual process when publishers bring foreign books to Korean readers.

I honestly didn't have a solid idea of what this process would look like, assuming maybe I would be involved in the process in one way or another. Even though my primary language is Korean, I left the country almost twenty years ago. I hardly ever communicate with anyone in Korean these days, nor do I write regularly in Korean, so my confidence in writing in Korean wasn't that high. However, there was a big worry in me at the same time whether the eventual Korean version of the book would be something I didn't recognize, as if it were written by someone else. Whenever I read a translated version of any book, I tend to feel a gap, as if something's missing from what the author intended. I always prefer reading in the language an author originally used.

I called the Korean publisher and asked if I could translate the book, at least the introduction, and see whether I was capable of this work, to begin with, and whether my version of the book would have a stronger connection to the reader than another translator's might.

After an initial trial, the Korean editor confirmed that she preferred my translated version of the book to that done by other translators, saying mine had a stronger pull and feeling of energy coming directly from the author. And that is how my journey of translating my book started about a month ago.

Interestingly, the more I worked on this project, the stronger I felt that this was indeed *my* job, not someone else's. I was completely rewriting the content in Korean and never directly translating from what I wrote in English. The book was recreated as something entirely new as it went through the same author's brain process in a different language, the author's own mother language.

What I have been experiencing in this process is something I've never expected: I was reconnecting with myself—my youth, the language, and the culture I grew up in. At first, I needed an

English–Korean dictionary for every ten words; then, soon, the flow of my primary language reappeared.

The work itself was very heavy, though. The volume of the book is not like a one-page article but a book more than 250 pages long! However, the Korean publishing company editor mentioned that in her history of working in this industry, this was the first time she had witnessed a foreign book translated into Korean by its original author.

I am very excited to share this book with Korean readers, and I am already thrilled by this process and what this has given me.

In my day-to-day life these days, whenever I feel overwhelmed by the workload and a tight deadline, I remind myself that I need to change the words from *have to* to *get to*. No, I don't *have to* translate my book. I *get to* translate my book, which is an amazing opportunity and privilege to me and my life.

Do you have anything pressing in your life right now? Can you switch from thinking of it as a chore and think of it as a privilege? Simply try to change your approach from *have to* to *get to*.

You don't *have to* exercise; you *get to* exercise. You don't *have to* work; you *get to* work.

I bet you'll gain a new perspective on what you do and will feel a deep sense of gratitude by simply changing those words.

Concert Corner

"Limoges, le marché" ("The Market at Limoges") from
Pictures at an Exhibition by Modest Mussorgsky

End of a Day by Jeonyeok ▶

JEONEOK

50.

We Need More Lazy Days

During the holiday season, as much as it feels a bit abnormal for me to have these days without an agenda, I am aware that we all need more lazy days. According to the famous Zen master Thich Nhat Hanh, a lazy day is a day for us to be without any scheduled activities. We just let the day unfold naturally, timelessly.

On this day, we have a chance to reestablish balance. We might go for a walk, read a book in a park or by the fireplace, dine with the family, write a card to a friend, or do a sitting meditation in nature. It can be a day to look deeply into our relationship with ourselves or with others. Or we may learn that we just need to rest. I remember those days when I came to my mom's house in Korea and spent days just sleeping—that feeling of being able to fully rest the mind and body at home, at last.

We are often wired to seek entertainment or feel uneasy about being bored constantly. Thich Nhat Hanh says, "A lazy day is a chance to train ourselves not to be afraid of doing nothing. You might think that not doing anything is a waste of time. But that's not true. Your time is first of all for you to be—to be alive, to be at peace. The world needs joyous and loving people who are capable of just being. People sometimes say, 'Don't just sit there; do something.' But we have to reverse that statement to say, 'Don't do something; just sit there' in order to be in such a way that peace, understanding, and compassion are possible."

May your life have more lazy days when you can calm your inner storm, fully be in touch with yourself, rest, don't think, and regenerate yourself so that you can be better equipped to be understanding and compassionate with the world and yourself.

Concert Corner

◀ "Catacombae" ("Catacombs") and "Cum Mortuis in Lingua Mortua" ("With the Dead in a Dead Language") from *Pictures at an Exhibition* by Modest Mussorgsky

Autumn by oc.ssc ▶

51.

The Emotional Journey of Retirement

Recently, I witnessed several people retire from their work. It seems like a coincidence that these milestone events occurred to many people I know around the same time. Because of this, I had the privilege of experiencing their transitions up close.

At the beginning of their retirement announcements about a year ago, each person seemed beyond excited and more than ready to start a relaxed pace of life. They were tired and ready to take the break they had been waiting for. Then, interestingly, close to the actual retirement date, there was much more of a sense of loss and sadness. It even came as a surprise to them. Although they were happy to move on, there was a grieving process of saying goodbye to their identities after doing that particular work for decades.

Last week, I attended a retirement party for a piano professor at a university where many former students gathered and celebrated his forty-five-year teaching career. Everyone shared their stories, expressed gratitude for having him as a teacher and mentor, and celebrated his achievements. Even though I hadn't studied with him, I felt conflicted emotions of sadness and joy for him. Strangely, it all felt like your own funeral that you could actually attend, listening to people's experiences of you in person. It was beautiful and nostalgic at the same time.

The professor shared his feelings with the attendees and said, "I've learned three things as a teacher. First, the ultimate goal of a teacher is to help students become independent thinkers. The less I was needed in the end, the better job I was doing in the process. Also, you need to have a sense of humor when teaching. Don't take everything too seriously. Lastly, teaching was the hardest yet the most rewarding job I've ever done in my life."

I couldn't help but imagine what my transition will look like in the future or what my funeral will look like. *What would people say about me?*

No matter what the profession was for all these new retirees, I sensed similarities between them, which made me reflect on several thoughts regarding retirement and life.

First, giving love and being of service to someone seem to be vital ingredients in feeling connected and fulfilled through one's career and beyond.

Second, it seems important to understand that the transition process is not as easy as they first perceived and is often emotional. Because of that, I found that those who reflect on their past and make a conscious effort to write or share their emotions with others seem to be healthier. Whether through a conversation with a close friend or a big retirement party, it seems good to reflect and embrace the loss of identity.

Last is a reminder that what you do is not who you are. I ask myself, *If I can't play piano anymore, can't teach piano anymore, or can't do anything I do currently anymore, does it mean I am not Jeeyoon?* Music makes me happy, and a musical life fits me well. However, Jeeyoon inside is the same no matter what I do as a profession. The idea that I am not what I do frees me from my own cocoon.

It is easy to attach to my identity as a pianist, but I will probably have to remind myself over and over again that I will always be who I am regardless.

Like Buddha said, "In the end, only three things matter: How much have you loved? How gently have you lived? How gracefully have you let go of things?"

Retirement is certainly a letting go of things, especially the thing we are the most attached to: our sense of self tied in with what we do professionally. Just like many life lessons, I find that letting go is one of the hardest to execute when it is most needed. It takes practice and encouragement within oneself.

A close friend of mine who has been retired for several years told me that she is the happiest she's ever been these days. What she enjoys the most is the slow morning routine, in which there is the freedom to design her own flow for the day.

Concert Corner

"The Hut on Fowl's Legs (Baba Yaga)" from *Pictures at an Exhibition* by Modest Mussorgsky

A Place Where Warmth Stays by Yoon Min Jeong (grimgrit)

52.

The Saturday Morning Test

One of the most fortunate things about my life has been that I've always known what the passion of my life is. I don't remember consciously choosing the piano when I was four years old, but I remember loving going to a piano institute every day, being that musical kid on the block. For me, there wasn't any moment in my life when I doubted that interest.

When I was a high school freshman, my dad once commented, "In this world, it would be much easier for you to make a living as a doctor or a pharmacist than a pianist. You are a smart girl; you will make a good doctor too." At that moment, I remember loud and clear in my head that there was no other way that I could be anything but a musician. I understood his reasoning: Thinking through the uncertainty of being an artist and making sure that I knew what I was headed for would be a good process, especially early on. Yes, the professional musical path is not for everyone. If anyone knows the hardship of this unknown music world, it is me. However, I didn't choose the music for being easy or difficult. I chose it because I knew that I was being true to my inner voice.

People often say that they wish they also knew what they wanted to do with their lives. As much as I am certain for now about what I love and it has been a focal point of my life, I doubt that anyone knows exactly what they want to do with their entire life. What is more important for us is to be aware, to listen to ourselves constantly throughout our lives, and to be able to navigate to our most authentic selves with that deep listening. I want to lead my life with that openness of being able to adjust as I transform myself as time goes by.

I believe that through openness and curiosity, I found many other interests to shine in my life, such as writing, creating podcasts, teaching piano, being the sole entrepreneur of my company, and understanding the landscape of the business world. One by one, these elements of interest knocked on my life door to invite me to get closer, and I walked toward it.

I love watching longboarding surfers walking on their boards, gliding on peeling waves. What I am most amazed at is that underneath their smooth and graceful movement, their feet are constantly moving and adjusting to the change of the waves. There is no still moment, even if it looks like they are simply gliding.

They listen to the waves and make micro-adjustments of weight distributions or small arm movements, or sometimes, they take a big step forward or backward.

Perhaps our lives are similar. We can't change how each wave (or moment in life) would behave, but we can always adapt our mind and body to the wave. If you stick with only one method, a certain wave knocks you down as you ignore what that particular wave is asking you to change.

Neil Pasricha, the author of *The Happiness Equation*, says that in order to find your passion, you need to keep asking questions about what would be a reason to get out of bed in the morning. He calls it the Saturday morning test: "What do you do on Saturday morning when you have nothing to do?"

Do you like gardening? Do you go to the gym? Do you play the guitar? Do you bake bread? I am sure there will be hundreds of possibilities. When you think about answering this simple question, take your time and answer it out loud. The answers might change day to day, but I find that they might give you various directions in which you can follow opportunities naturally drawn from the answers. This search doesn't have to yield professional work; simply keep it as a hobby. I am sure that this knowledge will make you happier by living your life by doing what you love.

Dale Carnegie reminds us, "Are you bored with life? Then throw yourself into some work you believe in with all your heart, live for it, die for it, and you will find happiness that you had thought could never be yours."

I hope this can help you to enrich your personal and work life. If anything, simply do more of what you love.

Life is short. But love is long.

Concert Corner

"The Great Gate of Kiev" from *Pictures at an Exhibition* by Modest Mussorgsky

In the Lush Silence
by Mclalan

Epilogue

When one of my concerts is over, I often have a case of the blues for days afterward. Even with the most successful concert, I feel the need to take a break and stay grounded alone for a while after the joyous musical celebration with everyone. The bigger the concert to prepare for, the deeper the void I feel afterward. Coming down from the mountain is often more complex than going up.

At most concerts, I come out to the lobby right after the concert to greet the audience members. We share a brief chat about our musical experience together. Audience members often tell me their favorite piece in the concert and share their appreciation. Sometimes, the line after the concert is so long that I end up staying for one or two hours in the lobby to greet everyone. People often worry that I might be too tired to be there or dread being there, but on the contrary, I absolutely cherish every second of that time. It feels like we just took a unique journey together and we need to digest it.

Finally, after the bright lights of the stage have been turned off, the piano is tucked off to the side, and the last person has left the greeting line, I go back to the greenroom to pack my few belongings and change from my concert dress to casual clothes.

Whenever I come outside from the concert hall, the ordinary scene of the night often seems like a bit of a shock to my system: people walking fast on a sidewalk with their briefcases tucked under their arms, lights inside restaurants flashing scenes of people dining, or a person wearing headphones waiting while his dog pees on a tree. Such typical city scenes look foreign to me, as if I had time traveled from two hundred years ago and landed right there without any prior warning.

Writing a book is a strangely similar process. After I finished the last sentence of the final chapter of this book, I felt a hint of sadness and joy mixed together. This journey was so exciting and personal that I felt the need to talk to someone to share the experience in an imaginary lobby.

Often, after a big concert, I take a week or two—or even months—during which I like not to think about when or what the next big musical project or concert will be. I take my time without doing much productive work. However, this book has been different in that regard. Even after sending the final manuscript of the book to the publisher, I have been writing continually and connecting with many of you through my biweekly newsletter,

Behind the Keys. I regularly showed up and shared myself with you through writing.

I am grateful that my relationship with you through words won't end here in this final chapter because there is another way to connect with you beyond the book. If you haven't, please join my biweekly newsletter via my website, www.jeeyoonkim.com, or follow this QR code to sign up directly:

If the timing is right, you might be able to catch me at one of my live piano concerts in your area. How exciting it would be to share music with you in person! Please say hello to me afterward, would you?

I am humbled and grateful to share this experience of *Beyond the Keys* with you.

I am curious about who I might become twenty or thirty years from now.

I am curious about how you will transform yourself.

I love this quote by Helena Bonham Carter: "I think everything in life is art. What you do. How you dress. The way you love someone and how you talk. Your smile and your personality. What you believe in, and all your dreams. The way you drink your tea. How you decorate your home. Or party. Your grocery list. The food you make. How your writing looks. And the way you feel. Life is art."

Let's continue this beautiful path of *becoming* in our lives.

I am grateful to share a moment on our life journeys—in front of the keys and beyond them.

Warmly,

Jeeyoon

Concert Corner

"10 More Minutes" by Jeeyoon Kim

About the Author

Award-winning classical pianist Jeeyoon Kim has delighted audiences across the United States and the world with her combination of sensitive artistry, "consummate musicianship, impeccable technique, and engaging and innovative concert experiences" (from the *New York Classical Review*).

From the start of her career, beginning with her celebrated 2016 debut album, *10 More Minutes*, Jeeyoon has thrilled classical music fans with her artful performances. Through her unique performance presentations, she has connected with concert attendees decidedly younger than the average by engaging in musical conversations from the stage. In her second album and concert project, *Over. Above. Beyond.*, Jeeyoon further stretched the mold for classical piano performances by collaborating with New York–based artist Moonsub Shin. Jeeyoon's collaboration with the artist delivered a multimedia experience captured in an award-winning music video featuring Coda alla Reminiscenza, Op. 38, No. 8 from *Forgotten Melodies* by Nikolai Medtner.

Jeeyoon's next project, titled 시음 */si-úm/* (poetry and music in Korean), began during her 2020 residency at the Banff Centre for Arts and Creativity for their *Concert in the 21st Century* program. This concert project incorporates poetry and black-and-white photography. Jeeyoon's dedication to pushing the boundaries of traditional classical music to connect with a new audience has inspired a dedicated and passionate fanbase.

Jeeyoon began studying the piano when she was four years old, and her love of music propelled her through her undergraduate studies in piano performance in her native Korea. After moving to the United States, she received her master of music and doctor of musical arts in piano performance, with distinction, from Indiana University's renowned Jacobs School of Music.

In pursuit of a deeper understanding of music education, she earned a second master's degree in piano pedagogy from Butler University, where she concurrently served as a faculty member. As a testament to Jeeyoon's abilities as an educator, she was recognized with the Top Music Teacher Award from Steinway & Sons for three consecutive years, from 2016 to 2018.

Jeeyoon has shared her fresh perspective on classical piano performance with audiences at beloved venues such as Carnegie Hall in New York City, the Chamber Music Society in San Francisco, and the Stradivari Society in Chicago. Her fast-growing podcast, *Journey Through Classical Piano*, is dedicated to helping people of all musical tastes and backgrounds discover the beauty of classical music. Its fifteen-minute episodes feature concert-like musical experiences and in-depth explorations of classical compositions.

Jeeyoon is an author, educator, public speaker, podcaster, and award-winning performer. In 2021, she published her first book, *Whenever You're Ready*, offering readers a personal glimpse into her life. This self-help book in a concert-style structure shares wisdom and insights gained from Jeeyoon's musical experiences. After a successful reception throughout North America and Europe, the book was published in South Korea in 2022 as *Millions of Dreams* (백만 번의 상상). The book, translated into Korean by the author herself, made it to the top three bestsellers in South Korea in the self-help category. She is also a co-author of the book *Ever the Beginning*, published in 2025.

Jeeyoon currently resides in San Diego. Beyond a busy concert touring schedule, she happily practices her piano daily and maintains a studio full of dedicated piano students. As the creative director of Kim & Kim Piano Academy, she teaches passionate adult piano students worldwide (www.kimandkimpiano.com). When weather permits, Jeeyoon surfs each morning at sunrise.

Please visit
www.JeeyoonKim.com for more information.

If this book inspired you, please pass it on
to someone you want to inspire.

Praise for *Beyond the Keys*

"*Beyond the Keys* is like a glorious bouquet of flowers chosen for its colors and enticing scent to enhance your day. The table of contents let me create a mini-retreat using a choose-your-own menu: by title, by artwork, by musical selection. Jeeyoon's stories are shared with humor and vulnerability. Her music invited me to linger in the beauty of art and sound. It brightened my day each time I picked it up. Drop your phone and enjoy this book!"

—Amy Brothers, teacher

"Ever the teacher, Jeeyoon Kim inspires us with life-affirming lessons and universal truths. With an engaging writing style, she weaves a tapestry of color, sound, and masterful storytelling, replete with empathy and authenticity. *Beyond the Keys* transports us deep into the author's lived experiences—awash with vibrant colors and steeped in timeless melodies. Do you remember what it felt like as a five-year-old listening to someone, maybe a parent, read a story to you? The words alone transported us off to a new adventure. But then we saw the illustrations and went beyond the words into a magical or mysterious place. We traveled even farther if the reader added sound effects or different voices. During those wonderful moments, we felt curious, hopeful, perhaps a bit scared . . . but always safe and loved. And we had a calm sense that all is right with the world. So it is with Jeeyoon's stories. Months, even years from now, we will not remember all the words she wrote, but we'll never forget how she made us feel. Bravo, Jeeyoon! We are blessed that you are in our world."

—Karen Thickstun, retired professor of piano pedagogy

"When you read these stories, you may think, 'Wow, Jeeyoon has had an eventful, interesting life.' But she really hasn't. Everything that has happened to her has happened to you or could happen to you. What makes *Beyond the Keys* special is how Jeeyoon looks at things, and what you can learn from them. Could reflecting on a beautiful painting or a Chopin nocturne help you put your own life and all that has happened to you into better focus? Try it—you might be surprised! One of our big problems today is fragmentation, made worse by digital "communication" and "social media." Jeeyoon doesn't tell you how to achieve greater wholeness; hers isn't a self-help book in that sense (thank goodness). Rather, it is an exemplary set of models you can use on your own route to coherence by reflecting on the journey of a sensitive person who has devoted her life to seeking The Whole."

—Paul J. Gudel, professor of law

"Jeeyoon's special gift is introducing you to music the same way she lives it—like telling a story, reliving the surprising, hilarious, and poignant moments with each listener." —Joseph Bercovici, pianist and chef

"I didn't expect a book to slow me down in the best way. I found myself savoring each essay, then listening to the music in complete stillness. What a thoughtful and moving creation."

—Noah Park, father and poet

"With each story, Jeeyoon offers a fresh perspective and gives an effortless, gentle nudge in the right direction—always leaving the reader feeling inspired and motivated to pursue their own dreams and goals. Stunning and often whimsical artwork, paired with thoughtfully chosen music that accompanies each story, makes this book both unique and beautiful."

—Igor Pandurski, violinist

"Each time I open this book, I feel more grounded. The music, the artwork, the words—it's my little ritual of calm." —Emily Torres, mom

"*Beyond the Keys* has become my daily delight. Each evening, I read one chapter—only one—so that this newfound journey doesn't end too soon. I take time to admire the painting, then settle into a peacefulness as I absorb that chapter's music. It has become a moment of colorful tranquility I now look forward to each day, always wondering what adventure Jeeyoon will take me on next."

—Suzi Dillon, forever-student

"This labor of love pulses with humanity, empathy, and the author's unique ability to weave gentle, thought-provoking stories that stay with you long after the final page." —John Corban, piano teacher

"*Beyond the Keys* is a true gem—a blend of Jeeyoon's heartfelt stories, stunning piano music, and thoughtful visual art. She invites you to pause, reflect, and connect with your own journey—with warmth, humor, and a deep understanding of human nature. It's a book you'll treasure and share for the rest of your life." —Dianne Lefferts, amateur pianist

"Jeeyoon's resilience, compassion, and positivity are inspiring. *Beyond the Keys* is yet another gift she shares with the world, alongside her artistry as a pianist. I'm grateful for the joy she brings through her music and words." —Clara Kyunghee

"*Beyond the Keys* is an intimate glimpse into the heart of a true artist seeking her truth in everyday life. Jeeyoon combines music, visual art, and the written word to recreate the synergetic energy that expands, explains, and explores the human spirit."

—Susan Kitterman, former artistic director,
New World Youth Symphony

"This beautiful book is a multisensory journey through Jeeyoon's life stories, stunning music, and vivid illustrations. Each chapter captures her reflections and growth, weaving together engaging stories and piano performances that stir the soul. I highly recommend *Beyond the Keys* for anyone who loves music and human connection."

—Cindy Parker, higher education professional

"Jeeyoon's combination of storytelling, music, and visual art is unlike anything I've experienced. I laughed, teared up, and felt genuinely inspired. It's the kind of book you keep on your nightstand."

—Carlos Lin, bookworm

"*Beyond the Keys* is a breath of fresh air. The pairing of music with each story makes the experience come alive. It reminded me of why I fell in love with the arts in the first place."

—Lena Parker

"Jeeyoon's essays always feel like catching up with a close friend. She shares not only her musical journey, but also meaningful life lessons and insights on cultural differences—something I truly appreciate as someone from South America. ¡Gracias, Jeeyoon!"

—Marco Fierro, Spanish instructor

"Jeeyoon's writing offers a window into her life, revealing the depth and qualities needed to be an artist. As a piano student, her words have been a guiding light on the path to artistry."

—Javier Correa, amateur pianist

"After hearing Jeeyoon's music at the Baroque on Beaver Festival in 2019, my mother, husband, and I became instant fans. We love how her music, podcast, and newsletter bring thoughtful reflections and shared moments of beauty and kindness."

—Shirley, Brian, and Davonne

"*Beyond the Keys* is a book that blends and stirs our emotions. Jeeyoon invites us, as part of the human family, to share our hearts in words, music, art, and life. She gives us the chance to give, receive, and interact in love."

—Stuart Yatsko, Great Falls, Montana

Names and Credits for Works of Art Included in *Beyond the Keys*

The cover illustration by Jedit (@9jedit)

The dedication art by Jeonyeok (@jeonyeok)

The typography for the dedication art by Damso Cali (@damso_calli)

1. *Free Spirits* by Jeonyeok (@jeonyeok)
2. *Silent Luminosity* by Kaoru Yamada (@yamada_kao_gram)
3. *The Last Dance* by Jeonyeok (@jeonyeok)
4. *The Potted Guardian* by Kaoru Yamada (@yamada_kao_gram)
5. *The Leafy Embrace* by Shin Jinho (@sunnyshino)
6. *Puppy Train Play* by Gobom (@gobom_illust)
7. *Verdant Tranquility* by Kaoru Yamada (@yamada_kao_gram)
8. *Play the Piano* by Jin Young Park (@hwnie702)
9. *Oh! Voyage* by Van (@van._.hada)
10. *In Reflection's Stillness, Always Found* by Shin Jinho (@sunnyshino)
11. *Beyond the Now, My Eyes Must Reach* by Shin Jinho (@sunnyshino)
12. *Riding the Keys, Riding the Waves* by Jack Soren (@jacksoren)
13. *Angry Charlie* by Selynn Lee (@selynndraws)
14. *Piano in the Window* by Kaoru Yamada (@yamada_kao_gram)

15. *The First Snow* by MOSLA (@mosla_greem)
16. *Under Starry Sky* by Shin Jinho (@sunnyshino)
17. *Where Festivities Bloom* by Shin Jinho (@sunnyshino)
18. *Things That Can Only Be Seen from Afar* by Nakseo Jaengi Kim (@nurimcrystal)
19. *A Snowy Path, Traced by Our Gaze* by Jeonyeok (@jeonyeok)
20. *Warmer than the Sun, Bigger than the Ocean* by Yoon Min Jeong (grimgrit) (@grim_grit)
21. *Good Morning Radio* by MOSLA (@mosla_greem)
22. *Hope III* by Jed Dorsey (@jeddorseyart)
23. *Twilight Together at Masian Beach* by Nana (@nanadori__)
24. *A Wish Lifted to the Stars* by Jeonyeok (@jeonyeok)
25. *To You Who Brighten My Day* by Gobom (@gobom_illust)
26. *When the Sky Holds the Sea* by Mclalan (@mclalan_)
27. *Even the Sunset Smiles upon Us* by Jeonyeok (@jeonyeok)
28. *Ocean Elegance* by Art Rider (@art__rider_)
29. *Lost in Conversation, Time Flew* By by oc.ssc (@oc.ssc)
30. *In Gentle Light* by Kaoru Yamada (@yamada_kao_gram)
31. *Even Nürnberg After a Meal* by Yeono (@i_am_yeono)
32. *Cradled by the Ocean* by Hye Park (@parkhye_n3)
33. *Mont* by Van (@van._.hada)
34. *Stay* by Van (@van._.hada)
35. *Christmas in June* by Yeono (@i_am_yeono)
36. *Bami and Dessert* by MOSLA (@mosla_greem)
37. *White Wave Village (Yeongdo)* by Yuni (@yuni_0010)
38. *Smile* by Hye Park (@parkhye_n3)

39. *The Tapestry of Us* by Hye Park (@parkhye_n3)
40. *The Soul of Porto* by Yuni (@yuni_0010)
41. *Embraced by Autumn* by Van (@van._.hada)
42. *Going Home* by Yuni (@yuni_0010)
43. *The Flowers Picked from the Garden* by MOSLA (@mosla_greem)
44. *Adorable Couple* by Nakseo Jaengi Kim (@nurimcrystal)
45. *Hello, Sweet Summer* by Hye Park (@parkhye_n3)
46. *A Cozy Winter* by Hye Park (@parkhye_n3)
47. *I Like Yellow* by J RYU (@jryu_art)
48. *Between the City and Stillness* by Mclalan (@mclalan_)
49. *End of a Day* by Jeonyeok (@jeonyeok)
50. *Autumn* by oc.ssc (@oc.ssc)
51. *A Place Where Warmth Stays* by Yoon Min Jeong (grimgrit) (@grim_grit)
52. *In the Lush Silence* by Mclalan (@mclalan_)

The Pianist Jeeyoon Kim by Kasiq Jungwoo (@kasiqjungwoo)

Author portrait by Kasiq Jungwoo (@kasiqjungwoo)

Front and back endpaper artwork by Moonsub Shin (@moonsub)

Bibliography

Abdaal, Ali. *Feel-Good Productivity: How to Do More of What Matters to You* (Celadon, 2023).

Allen, David. *Getting Things Done: The Art of Stress-Free Productivity* (Penguin, 2001).

Bartlett, Steven. *The Diary of a CEO: The 33 Laws of Business and Life* (Portfolio, 2023).

Biss, Jonathan. "The Myth of the Mad Artist Is Harmful. I Should Know." *The New York Times* (October 30, 2024).

Dicks, Matthew. *Someday Is Today: 22 Simple, Actionable Ways to Propel Your Creative Life* (New World, 2022).

Dicks, Matthew. *Storyworthy: Engage, Teach, Persuade, and Change Your Life Through the Power of Storytelling* (New World Library, 2018).

Duhigg, Charles. *The Power of Habit: Why We Do What We Do in Life and Business* (Random House, 2014).

Forte, Tiago. *Building a Second Brain: A Proven Method to Organize Your Digital Life and Unlock Your Creative Potential* (Simon Element, 2022).

Gilbert, Elizabeth. *Big Magic: Creative Living Beyond Fear* (Riverhead, 2015).

Godin, Seth. *The Practice: Shipping Creative Work* (Portfolio, 2020).

Goldin, Leonid. "A Little Light in the Dark." *New Continent* (June 13, 2023).

Gottman, John, and Nan Silver. *The Seven Principles for Making Marriage Work: A Practical Guide from the Country's Foremost Relationship Expert* (Harmony Books, 2015).

Grant, Adam. *Think Again: The Power of Knowing What You Don't Know* (Viking, 2021).

Hanh, Thich Nhat. *How to Relax* (Parallax Press, 2015).

Jeffers, Susan. *Feel the Fear . . . and Do It Anyway: Dynamic Techniques for Turning Fear, Indecision, and Anger into Power, Action, and Love* (Harcourt, 1987).

Kirsch, Melissa. "The Post-Vacation Clarity." *The New York Times* (August 19, 2023).

McNee, Amie. "Unleashing Your Creative Magic: 7 Reasons Why Artists Enter Competitions." *Louise Hancox Fine Art* (August 29, 2023).

Pasricha, Neil. *The Happiness Equation: Want Nothing + Do Anything = Have Everything* (Putnam, 2016).

Perdian, Rick. "The Musical and Personal Are Closely Twined with Pianist Jeeyoon Kim." *New York Classical Review* (June 8, 2023).

Perkins, Bill. *Die with Zero: Getting All You Can with Your Money and Your Life* (Mariner, reprint, 2021).

Rubin, Gretchen. *The Happiness Project, Tenth Anniversary Edition: Or, Why I Spent a Year Trying to Sing in the Morning, Clean My Closets, Fight Right, Read Aristotle, and Generally Have More Fun* (Harper, 2019).

Ruiz, Don Miguel. *The Four Agreements: A Practical Guide to Personal Freedom* (Amber-Allen, 1997).

Sivers, Derek. *Hell Yeah or No: What's Worth Doing* (Hit Media, 2022).

Walker, Matthew. *Why We Sleep: Unlocking the Power of Sleep and Dreams* (Scribner, 2017).

Published by Greenleaf Book Group Press
Austin, Texas
www.gbgpress.com

Distributed by Greenleaf Book Group

For ordering information or special discounts for bulk purchases, please contact Greenleaf Book Group at PO Box 91869, Austin, TX 78709, 512.891.6100.

Design and composition by Greenleaf Book Group
Cover design by Jedit

Publisher's Cataloging-in-Publication data is available.

Print ISBN: 979-8-88645-362-1

eBook ISBN: 979-8-88645-363-8

To offset the number of trees consumed in the printing of our books, Greenleaf donates a portion of the proceeds from each printing to the Arbor Day Foundation. Greenleaf Book Group has replaced over 50,000 trees since 2007.

Printed in Canada on acid-free paper

25 26 27 28 29 30 31 10 9 8 7 6 5 4 3 2 1

First Edition

Free Spirits by Jeonyeok (@jeonyeok)

Silent Luminosity by Kaoru Yamada (@yamada_kao_gram)

The Last Dance by Jeonyeok (@jeonyeok)

The Potted Guardian by Kaoru Yamada (@yamada_kao_gram)

The Leafy Embrace by Shin Jinho (@sunnyshino)

Puppy Train Play by Gobom (@gobom_illust)

Verdant Tranquility by Kaoru Yamada (@yamada_kao_gram)

Play the Piano by Jin Young Park (@hwnie702)

Oh! Voyage by Van (@van._.hada)

In Reflection's Stillness, Always Found by Shin Jinho (@sunnyshino)

Beyond the Now, My Eyes Must Reach by Shin Jinho (@sunnyshino)

Riding the Keys, Riding the Waves by Jack Soren (@jacksoren)

Angry Charlie by Selynn Lee (@selynndraws)

Piano in the Window by Kaoru Yamada (@yamada_kao_gram)

The First Snow by MOSLA (@mosla_greem)

Under Starry Sky by Shin Jinho (@sunnyshino)

Where Festivities Bloom by Shin Jinho (@sunnyshino)

Things That Can Only Be Seen from Afar by Nakseo Jaengi Kim (@nurimcrystal)

A Snowy Path, Traced by Our Gaze by Jeonyeok (@jeonyeok)

Warmer than the Sun, Bigger than the Ocean by Yoon Min Jeong (grimgrit) (@grim_grit)

Good Morning Radio by MOSLA (@mosla_greem)

Hope III by Jed Dorsey (@jeddorseyart)

Twilight Together at Masian Beach by Nana (@nanadori__)

A Wish Lifted to the Stars by Jeonyeok (@jeonyeok)

To You Who Brighten My Day by Gobom (@gobom_illust)

When the Sky Holds the Sea by Mclalan (@mclalan_)

Even the Sunset Smiles upon Us by Jeonyeok (@jeonyeok)

Ocean Elegance by Art Rider (@art__rider_)

Lost in Conversation, Time Flew By by oc.ssc (@oc.ssc)

In Gentle Light by Kaoru Yamada (@yamada_kao_gram)

Even Nürnberg After a Meal by Yeono (@i_am_yeono)

Cradled by the Ocean by Hye Park (@parkhye_n3)

Mont by Van (@van._.hada)

Stay by Van (@van._.hada)

Christmas in June by Yeono (@i_am_yeono)

Bami and Dessert by MOSLA (@mosla_greem)

White Wave Village (Yeongdo) by Yuni (@yuni_0010)

Smile by Hye Park (@parkhye_n3)

The Tapestry of Us by Hye Park (@parkhye_n3)

The Soul of Porto by Yuni (@yuni_0010)

Embraced by Autumn by Van (@van._.hada)

Going Home by Yuni (@yuni_0010)

The Flowers Picked from the Garden by MOSLA (@mosla_greem)

Adorable Couple by Nakseo Jaengi Kim (@nurimcrystal)

Hello, Sweet Summer by Hye Park (@parkhye_n3)

A Cozy Winter by Hye Park (@parkhye_n3)

I Like Yellow by J RYU (@jryu_art)

Between the City and Stillness by Mclalan (@mclalan_)

End of a Day by Jeonyeok (@jeonyeok)

Autumn by oc.ssc (@oc.ssc)

A Place Where Warmth Stays by Yoon Min Jeong (grimgrit) (@grim_grit)

In the Lush Silence by Mclalan (@mclalan_)